LADDER
FOCUS

LADDER
FOCUS

creating, sustaining, and enlarging >YOUR BIG PICTURE

SAMUEL R. CHAND + GERALD BROOKS

HIGHLAND PARK, ILLINOIS

© 2007 by Samuel R. Chand
All rights reserved.

Printed in the United States of America

Published by:
Mall Publishing
641 Homewood Avenue
Highland Park, Illinois 60035
877.203.2453

Cover design by Worship Through the Arts
www.worshipthroughthearts.com

ISBN: 1-934165-31-X

Scripture references are from the following versions:

KJV: King James Version.

MSG: Scripture quotations from THE MESSAGE. Copyright © by Eugene H. Peterson 1993, 1994, 1995, 1996, 2000, 2001, 2002. Used by permission of NavPress Publishing Group.

NIV: Scripture quotations are taken from the Holy Bible, New International Version®. NIV®. Copyright © 1973, 1978, 1984 by International Bible Society.
Used by permission of Zondervan.
All rights reserved.

For licensing / copyright information, for additional copies or for use in specialized settings contact:

Dr. Samuel R. Chand

950 Eagles Landing Parkway, Suite 295
Stockbridge, GA 30281
www.samchand.com

Also by Samuel R. Chand

Failure:
The Womb of Success

Futuring:
Leading Your Church Into Tomorrow

Who's Holding Your Ladder?
Selecting Your Leaders—
Leadership's Most Critical Decision

Who Moved Your Ladder?
Your Next Bold Move

What's Shakin' Your Ladder?
15 Challenges *All* Leaders Face

Ladder*Shifts:*
New Realities, Rapid Change, Your Destiny

For more information:
Samuel R. Chand Ministries
950 Eagles Landing Parkway
Suite 250
Stockbridge, GA 30281
www.samchand.com

Also by Gerald Brooks

What I Learned While Destroying a Church

Paul on Leadership

The Old Testament on Leadership

Building Blocks of Leadership

The Emotions of a Leader

For more information:
Gerald Brooks
Grace Outreach Center
5000 Parker Road
Plano, TX 75093
972-985-1112
www.growingothers.com

Table of Contents

Foreword

Every successful leader I've ever known has possessed passion and vision. But not every person with passion and vision becomes a successful leader. What makes the difference? Leadership! That's why I say that everything rises and falls on leadership.

My two friends and colleagues, Gerald Brooks and Sam Chand, understand that. They are both highly effective leaders who are putting their passion and vision to work making a difference in this world. I have enjoyed the gift of their friendship for many years and have benefited from their wisdom as they have partnered with me in training millions of leaders around the world through EQUIP™. Now you will have the opportunity to benefit from their insight and wisdom.

Gerald and Sam are both gifted teachers, as well as leaders. In this book, they have assembled an essential guide to help equip church leaders so that their passion and vision become reality. In these pages, you will gain knowledge and understanding that will help you to communicate your vision, build bridges with people, and use your influence to advance God's kingdom where He has placed you.

Every time you improve as a leader, you are taking an important step forward in fulfilling the purpose God has given you. Keep running the race!

May God bless you as you serve Him in leadership.

John C. Maxwell
Founder, INJOY Stewardship Services and EQUIP

The Ladder Story
by Dr. Samuel R Chand

Waiting for someone to call me into the sanctuary, I stared out the window. As I meditated on the points I wanted to cover as a featured speaker at this conference, something in the street below caught my attention.

A man stood on a ladder painting—not that uncommon a sight. I smiled, remembering my student days in Bible college. I had spent my summers doing that kind of work. Yet I couldn't take my eyes off the man. For several minutes, I watched

> Old ladder holders are rarely adequate at holding new ladders.

his graceful motions as he moved his brush and roller across the surface.

As I watched, I noticed that this painter was only covering a limited area. He stretched as far as he could to the left, to the right and even reached above his head. It also occurred to me that he was only going to the height that he was comfortable at, even though the extension ladder he was using could reach much higher.

From my painting experience, I remembered that once I was on the ladder and had the necessary resources, I painted a much larger area before taking the additional time needed to climb down and relocate the ladder. It was an efficient method.

"Why isn't he going higher to paint all the way up? What would allow him to go higher?" I asked myself. Then I saw the reason—no one was holding his ladder. By himself, the painter couldn't go any further. He had done everything he could by himself. He needed help.

As I watched his graceful strokes, I realized the leadership parallels. Whether we're talking about churches, businesses or non-profit organizations, the effectiveness of a leader depends on the person or persons holding the ladder—those who are in support roles.

The height that a visionary leader reaches on the ladder to their vision is not controlled by the leader's capabilities. It's not even controlled by how inspiring their vision might be. It's controlled by who's holding the ladder.

Then another thought struck me: Those who hold the ladders are just as important as the leaders themselves.

The visionaries could have all the training possible, the most expensive equipment, years of experience and knowledge about painting, and a blend of expertise and passion about their craft. But that's not the deciding factor. The ladder holder determines the height to which the ladder climber ascends. "That's it!" I cried aloud. "Those who hold the ladder control the ascent of the visionaries."

> The height that a visionary leader reaches on the ladder to their vision is not controlled by the leader's capabilities.

Additionally, a ladder holder who may be very capable with a 20-foot extension ladder (or vision) may not be the person you want holding your 45-foot extension ladder (a new or enlarged vision). Old ladder holders are rarely adequate at holding new ladders.

My book, *Who's Holding Your Ladder?*, explains this powerful concept. It explains the need for qualified ladder holders and the necessary qualifications, differentiates between leaders and managers, and describes how you can turn your ladder holders into ladder climbers.

For other *Ladder* books and information,
visit **www.samchand.com**

The Sweetwater Story
by Dr. Gerald Brooks

We all make mistakes. We all have those moments that we wish we could redo. How marvelous it would be if life had a rewind button that allowed us to travel back before a mistake occurred and live the moment over again. We tell ourselves that this time we'd get it right.

Many of the lessons that I share at conferences across the country began during such a time in my life, during a period that I wish I could do over. When other pastors hear about Grace Outreach Center, the church that I currently pastor, many regard it as a huge success. They don't understand that Grace Outreach Center isn't the first church that I've pastored, that our success came at a price.

My first congregation doesn't exist anymore. The building where I held services is now the city dog pound for Sweetwater, Texas. Helping to ensure that fewer stray dogs roam the streets of Sweetwater isn't the lasting impact I wanted to leave on that city. Certainly, I wasn't trying to destroy the church; I was doing the best work that I could and praying for an increase in God's kingdom. But it happened. While I can't go back and fix it, I thank God that I've learned from the mistakes that I've made. Those lessons helped build Grace Outreach Center.

You don't have to make massive mistakes to miss your destination. If an airplane flying from Dallas to Austin makes a .5-degree navigational error on take-off, it seems like a minor error. However, that "little mistake" will have you landing in San Antonio. A lot of major errors appear minor at their inception.

I missed my desired destination in Sweetwater. But I learned the value of making good mistakes. Good mistakes are ones we learn and grow from; good mistakes give us lessons to share with others.

Everybody drops the ball at some point. The problem occurs when we continue the same pattern of mistakes. We need the humility and the wisdom to quickly recognize our blunders. If we don't see them, we're destined to repeat them.

While our God is a God of second chances, not many ministers are open to honestly sharing their mistakes. It's not that we're dishonest; we just have a "don't ask, don't tell" mentality. Someone has to ask very pointed questions before we're willing to talk about our missteps. In our church programs for future leaders, we work at providing them with these lessons, even though they're unable to fully appreciate them today. One day, when faced with similar problems, they'll know what to do.

I don't travel around the country to speak to other pastors because I pastor a successful church in Plano. I certainly don't do it because I need the work. I go because I remember what it feels like to have 70 people attend a church and to watch that number dwindle. I remember clearly what it feels like to stand up and preach to another empty seat every week. I remember what it feels like to have people slowly stop trusting and valuing you.

At the time, I wished that someone would help me turn things around. I knew the ship was sinking but I couldn't figure out what was causing it and there was no one offering to help me. I promised God that if I were fortunate enough to pastor a successful church one day, I would remember Sweetwater and I would help others.

Sweetwater is what compels me to share.

For other books by Dr. Gerald Brooks,
visit **www.growingothers.com**

Personal Focus:
How to Keep Your Heart in the Game

The path of the righteous is like the first gleam of dawn,
shining ever brighter till the full light of day.
-- Proverbs 4:18 (New International Version)

"Maybe I'm starting to backslide," Pastor Keith wondered aloud. The silence at the kitchen table was quickly shattered by his wife's familiar laughter. "Sure, Keith," exclaimed Ellen. "I can see the headlines now!" Rising slightly in her chair, she stopped laughing long enough to pull off an amazing imitation of the local TV news anchor, complete with a grocery list doubling as a script.

"After nearly 20 years of faithful ministry, popular local pastor Keith Hunt has reportedly succumbed to the **powerful** temptation of running his father's **nearly bankrupt** business. Unnamed church officials told this reporter they wonder if he has actually backslidden or has simply taken leave of his senses." Exploding with fresh laughter, she reached across the table and squeezed his hand, her smile radiating.

Ellen's eye for irony never failed to lift Keith's spirits; he could always count on her for perspective. Yes, he was considering leaving a thriving pastorate. Yes, he wanted to run his father's ailing business. He'd thought about barely anything else for months, ever since assisting the company while his dad recovered from surgery. He'd always loved his dad's work. During his recent time there, Keith developed a deeper admiration for the people who worked for his dad and nimbly developed ideas to revive its once-thriving business, ideas that surprised him. It wasn't something he planned; it just happened.

He prayed and fasted about his changing passions, yet no clear direction emerged. Soon after, his dad began talking of retiring and asked Keith to consider running the family business. Staring into Ellen's smiling face, Keith was troubled by two nagging questions: what to tell his dad and what to tell his church.

Do you find yourself in a situation similar to Pastor Keith's? Perhaps you're feeling pulled in a new direction lately. Maybe you're sensing a change in the wind or finding different dreams occupying your thoughts. If so, we have encouraging news for you: You don't have to be afraid to make a transition.

It's perfectly normal for your focus to shift. When it happens, be honest with yourself. There are some of you who might be in ministry now who might need to either return to – or perhaps enter – the business world because you'll have a greater Godly influence there. Some of you might be going from the secular arena into ministry. Both are valid shifts. It's important to remember that you are *always* in ministry regardless of where

> It's perfectly normal for your focus to shift.

you are. No one should narrowly define full-time ministry only as leaving a secular job to go preach somewhere. Was Paul any less of an apostle when he was making tents?

Maybe you've heard friends or acquaintances in the ministry say things like, "I wish I could go back to developing houses," "I dream about going back into the banking industry," or "I really want to take a new opportunity in sales." Many times, when pastors say things like this, they're viewing these moves as regressive. However, that's not always the case. Making a transition doesn't have to be regressive; it can be a step into freedom.

There are many leaders who feel trapped where they are, who let themselves be governed by circumstances and situations, even though God may be opening another door for them. If you're sensing that God might be making a shift in your life, go ahead and catch that wave. Keep your focus, trust God to provide, and ensure your freedom by making sure that all of your dealings are conducted with Godly integrity.

> Making a transition doesn't have to be regressive; it can be a step into freedom.

In this chapter, we'll examine the ways that God might be leading you, talk about how to handle your shifting passions, and share how you can maintain your focus.

Discovering How God Guides You

For Moses, it was a burning bush. For the Apostle Paul, it was an experience on Damascus Road. For Joseph, it was an understanding of dreams. God speaks to each of us differently, communicating His message in different ways. That's why it's important to know how God tends to speak to you.

Tim Elmore, president of growingleaders.com, talks about different ways that God speaks to his servants. Here are the five major methods God uses to speak to us:

1. Being called from birth
2. A thunderbolt
3. Open doors
4. Growing awareness
5. Obedience to a Scriptural mandate

1. **Being called from birth** is defined in Jeremiah 1:5, "Before I formed you in the womb I knew you; before you were born I set you apart." Jesus, John the Baptist, and the prophet Jeremiah are just some examples of people who were set apart by God at an early age.

2. When God sent **a thunderbolt** to Saul on Damascus Road, it changed his life's direction.

Dr. Brooks' Experience

I experienced a similar, but somewhat less dramatic call from the Lord. While I always knew that I should be in ministry, I wasn't sure about the specifics. After six hours of praying in a local park, God spoke to me clearly about pastoring in Plano, Texas, as well as the specific area of town he wanted me in. And God confirmed this guidance in a number of ways.

3. One of the ways that God speaks to Dr. Chand is through **open doors**.

Dr. Chand's Experience

When I sense that seizing an opportunity would please the Lord, I simply do it. If the situation doesn't work out, I know I can always end it. However, I won't know which way the opportunity will go unless I say "yes."

4. **Growing awareness** is another way in which Dr. Chand receives guidance.

Dr. Chand's Experience

I cannot point to a day and time when God lead me into this current work of consulting with high-impact organizations and developing leaders. I began working with leaders while still running Beulah Heights Bible College. As more and more leaders asked for my help, I became aware that this ministry was shifting into a new phase and I would have to leave the college.

5. Some leaders are simply led through their **obedience to a Scriptural mandate**. Knowing that they should be feeding the poor, caring for the sick, or preaching the good news is all the guidance that some leaders need. For example, someone once asked Mother Te-

resa when she was called to minister in Calcutta. She responded, "I was never called. I saw a need and thought I could help."

Regardless of how He speaks to you – whether it's one method or a combination – God knows the most effective way to communicate His plan to you. Some of it has to do with your personality. Some people are just more attuned to subtleties, which means they'll respond to a growing awareness. Others might need to get whacked by a divine sledgehammer or a hit with thunderbolt. The more intense your personality, the more direct God has to be with you.

> God speaks to each of us differently, communicating His message in different ways. That's why it's important to know how God tends to speak to you.

Think back to the times in your life when God has guided you. How has He communicated? While God is certainly not limited, chances are that He'll use similar means now. And once He provides the guidance you need, it will be an anchor that will keep you stable through tough times and during difficult days.

Handling Internal Shifts

Sometimes, pastors and leaders experience restlessness or may intuitively recognize that things are about to change before they can even articulate what they're sensing. They struggle simply because their leadership gifts enable them to sense change before others see it.

Because navigating these ambiguous changes can involve

so many unknowns, it's important that you have some constants, some things that are non-negotiable. That's where your value system comes in. Even in the midst of change, you must always know that some things cannot be negotiated.

In addition to involving your faith, navigating internal shifts also relies heavily upon your intuition. Don't underestimate the importance of your intuition in navigating these internal changes. God will use your intuition to speak to you. For example, let's say you were talking with another pastor friend who was telling you about the new areas that he wants to move into. In the process, you learn that he's planning to totally discard everything that God had done in his life until then. Wouldn't your intuition flash a warning sign?

> Even in the midst of change, you must always know that some things cannot be negotiated.

It's your intuition that tells you that whatever shifting is going on will enhance the wisdom and experience that God has enabled you to accumulate over the years. It's your intuition that enables you to see how God is building upon your experiences to expand your ministry, to take you to different places. It's your intuition that will keep you from heading into dangerous places – like ignoring the legacy and values that God has established in your life.

When Bill Hybels talks about the intuitive leader, he describes someone who picks up on things from the inside, at a gut level. He reminds us of the Old Testament story where David knew God was moving by listening for the breeze ruffling the leaves of the mulberry tree[1]. When we talk about intuition, we're talking about listening to the subtleties of what God is saying in our hearts. God wants to lead us; He doesn't want to force us.

Unfortunately, experience is often the enemy of intuition. When you've been in ministry and leadership for a while, it's easy for your intuitive sensors to become corroded, for you to begin brushing things off. All day long, people are giving you ideas or sharing their pain. It's often too easy to become calloused and cynical.

> **God wants to lead us; He doesn't want to force us.**

Here are some ideas that will help you to keep your antenna up so that you can intuitively hear the subtleties of God:

- Get a prayer life
- Invest in stillness
- Be clear about what's important

Get a prayer life. Having a *prayer life* is very different from having a *prayer list.* Dr. Brooks has had to learn to distinguish between the two.

Dr. Brooks' Experience

As a pastor, I'm aware of hundreds of needs and am told about hundreds of problems. I've had to train myself to look at those hundreds of concerns and say, "These are things I'm praying for; that's my prayer list. But I can't let my prayer list become my prayer life."

Sometimes, it has to be just us and God. We don't have to come seeking anything; it's enough just to spend time together. Sometimes, it's not about praying for something to happen; it's about spending time in prayerful meditation.

An easy way to get started: simply take specific promises from Scripture and pray about them. For example, Ephesians 1 says that God has given us the spirit of wisdom and revelation in the knowledge of Him, so that the eyes of our understanding would be enlightened[2]. By praying like this, we're not spending all of our time praying about the things that are around us, but praying about the things God wants to accomplish within us.

...experience is often the enemy of intuition.

Invest in stillness. Too many leaders lead hectic lives. Too many of us get our self-worth from how busy we are and brag about the demands on our time.

In his book *Crazy Busy*, psychiatrist Edward Hallowell takes the insights he's gained in treating kids with attention-deficit disorder (ADD) and applies them to his friends, acquaintances and the world around him. He says that many of us exhibit the same characteristics as children with ADD. In fact, he says that so many of us are so overextended that our entire society appears to be suffering from "culturally induced ADD."

Sometimes, it has to be just us and God.

Unfortunately, pastors and church leaders are not exempt from Hallowell's charge. The greatest need of today's leaders might be to seek the fulfillment of Psalm 46:10, "be still and know that I am the Lord."

Each of us needs to find that place of inner stillness, that place where we're at rest, that place that invites God to speak. We have to fight to be still. We need to dim the lights and stop the activity so that we can simply sense His presence.

Be clear about what's important. In the midst of a world that wants to occupy us with a thousand non-essential things, we have to be focused on the heart of ministry. And being overwhelmed by the *activity* of ministry doesn't mean that you have the *heart* of ministry.

> We have to fight to be still.

In *Crazy Busy*, Hallowell recalls a conversation he had with a professional juggler. He asked the juggler, "What's the most you've ever seen someone juggle?" While the juggler had once seen someone juggle nine items, he'd never successfully juggled more than six. When Hallowell suggested that he try juggling seven things, the juggler had a very interesting reply. "I can awe my audience by juggling six things; I don't need to juggle seven." Because the juggler understood how much additional practice and work it would take him to juggle one additional item, he quickly concluded that the return on this investment just didn't justify it.

That's exactly what each of us has to determine: How many things has God called us to juggle? Are we beginning to juggle things that we don't need to be juggling? Are we trying to keep six things in the air when we're only called to handle four? Do we have a clear set of priorities that enables us to say, "I don't have to juggle everything that everyone's asking me to juggle." Are we secure enough in our calling that we know that we can have

> ...being overwhelmed by the activity of ministry doesn't mean that you have the heart of ministry.

a successful ministry juggling six things even though there are mega-churches juggling 11 things?

Clearing the interference from your intuitive antennae can provide your ministry with clear direction and help you to navigate internal shifts. Think about the times you've been driving on the highway, stuck behind an 18-wheeler. When you're behind one of these big rigs, it's difficult to see what's coming. But once you've moved into an open lane, you can clearly see the road again. That's exactly where God wants us – in that open lane where our hearts are open and ready to hear from Him afresh.

> How many things has God called us to juggle?

Maintaining Your Focus

Being productive while you're navigating personal change is difficult. While your heart may be yearning for a different place, you still have services to conduct and duties to perform. It's the daily demands of ministry that cause many leaders to simply ignore their own shifting passions and press on. Rather than stuffing what we're feeling, we need to respond with wisdom and courage. To do that, we need the support and encouragement of trusted friends.

> Being productive while you're navigating personal change is difficult.

We have both relied upon this Biblical principle during our personal times of transition.

> ## Our Experiences
>
> - Dr. Chand: *When I was in the midst of the changes that lead to leaving my post as college president, I sought the advice of my own inner circle.*
>
> - Dr. Brooks: *I relied upon my board to independently confirm the call to pastor that I heard while praying.*

Please don't hesitate to talk with your friends. If they're good friends, they'll welcome the opportunity to discuss your situation. In fact, your friends are probably already witnessing the subtle shifts you may think you're keeping so well hidden. If they come to you before you approach them, don't be threatened; welcome them in openness.

During World War II, our intelligence people used multiple points to determine where a radio signal originated. By triangulating these signals, they could figure out where an enemy target was. Today, our friends can help us to distinguish whether the signals we're getting are something new that God is saying to us, or whether it's just a tough time that we need to walk through.

Too often, people let situations determine their destiny. We all know that pastors are not immune to this. Rather than reacting to situations, we can get wisdom by following the Scriptural principle of submitting to others[3]. Submission has to be a quality found in every leader. In his series on Dynamic Deliverers, Jack Hayford describes how even after Moses received his charge from God at the burning bush, he

> ...we need others to help us determine if what we're hearing is just us, if it's a bad time in our life, or we've just walked into "a God moment."

submitted his experience and his plans to his father-in-law, his wife and his brother. Every leader needs to have that balance; we need others to help us determine if what we're hearing is just us, if it's a bad time in our life, or we've just walked into "a God moment."

Maintaining our focus is also easier when we're concentrating on positives rather than negatives. Focus is the key to all ministry. Like the Apostle Paul, we should be able to say, "This one thing I do.[4]" When we are sensing upcoming transitions, it should be because God is enlarging our vision, because the love for a new direction growing within us is eclipsing our love for where we are. It should be

> Focus is the key to all ministry.

because God is expanding our mission and skill set, not because we've become weary in well doing or because we're responding to something negative about where we are.

It's vital that we're honest with ourselves about our motives. All leadership comes from the heart and people always respond to the heart of a leader. If they sense the heart of a shepherd, they'll be drawn to your ministry. That's why 1 Peter talks about not leading grudgingly or out of necessity[5]. We have to do what we do willingly. Too many times, we stay in a position out of necessity simply because we need a paycheck. If your heart is not in what you're doing, integrity requires that you move on.

Maintaining your integrity is an essential part of navigating a personal transition. We've all heard of people in business who are only treading water until a better opportunity comes along, who are biding their time until retirement, or about folks who show up for work each day while their hearts and minds are elsewhere. There's no doubt that this type of behavior can harm a business. When this behavior comes from a church leader, the results can be devastating.

This disparity in results is easily explained. In the business world, what you produce is tied to *what you do*. Business leaders produce cheaper products, better products, or higher service. In the church, leaders reproduce *who they are*. The church is about character, it's about integrity, and it's about your heart. If a leader's heart is elsewhere, what are they reproducing?

> You can doubt yourself and trust God simultaneously.

Deciding to pull the trigger can be scary. However, if you're moving in faith and discerning a shift that's of God, you can trust that He has every detail planned. Dr. Chand witnessed this in the timing of his departure from Beulah Heights Bible College.

Dr. Chand's Experience

At the time, I had no idea if this consulting work would equal my paycheck from the college, but I knew it was time to move on. Still, it took faith for me to approach the chairman of the board to tender my resignation. In my book, *Who Moved Your Ladder*, I described the co-existence of God's direction and my inner angst. You can doubt yourself and trust God simultaneously.

Integrity also requires that we transition our position in order. We should focus on performing our duties to the best of our ability and easing the transition of whoever succeeds us. It might involve selecting or mentoring a successor. Our goal should always be to leave our current organization in better condition than it was in when we arrived, with healthy people that we've prepared to carry on God's work.

In the opening of this chapter, we quoted the Proverb that says, *"The path of the righteous grows brighter and brighter."* None of us needs to feel trapped in our current situation. If God is enlarging our vision, we can depend upon Him to lead us. When He is

None of us needs to feel trapped in our current situation.

calling to our hearts to shift lanes, we can trust Him to make our path clearer. It's going to require faith, but the result of that faith will conform us into the brightness of His image.

Teaching Points

- It's perfectly normal for your focus to shift. When it happens, be honest with yourself.
- If you're sensing that God might be making a shift in your life, keep your focus, trust God to provide, and ensure that all of your dealings are conducted with Godly integrity.
- God speaks to each of us differently, communicating His message in different ways. That's why it's important to know how God tends to speak to you.
  - Being called from birth
  - A thunderbolt
  - Open doors
  - Growing awareness
  - Obedience to a Scriptural mandate
- Think back to the times in your life when God has guided you. How has He communicated?
- Because navigating these ambiguous changes can involve so many unknowns, it's important that you have some constants, some things that are non-negotiable.
- Don't underestimate the importance of your intuition in navigating these internal changes. God will use your intuition to speak to you.
- It's easy for your intuitive sensors to become corroded after being in leadership for a while.
- To keep your antenna up so that you can intuitively hear the subtleties of God:
  - Get a prayer life. Don't let a prayer list become your prayer life.
  - Invest in stillness. Find that place of inner stillness, that place where we're at rest, that place that invites God to speak.

- Be clear about what's important. Don't let the activity of ministry keep us from the heart of ministry.
- Rather than stuffing feelings and pressing on with daily demands of ministry, we should seek to talk with friends.
- Our friends can help us determine whether we're hearing something new from God or whether it's a tough time we need to walk through.
- Submitting to others is a Scriptural principle.
- If we're considering moving on, it should be because the love for a new direction is eclipsing the love for where we are.
- Maintaining integrity is essential in navigating a personal transition.
    - Leaders produce who they are. If their hearts are elsewhere, what are they reproducing?
    - Integrity requires leading our position in order.

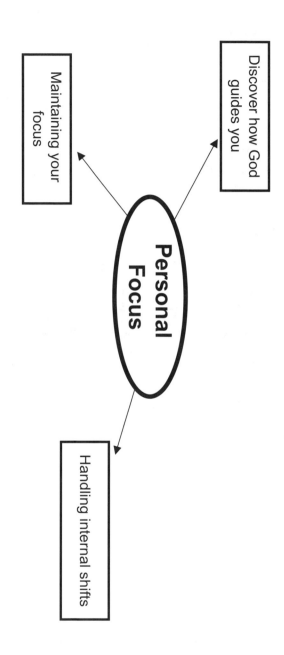

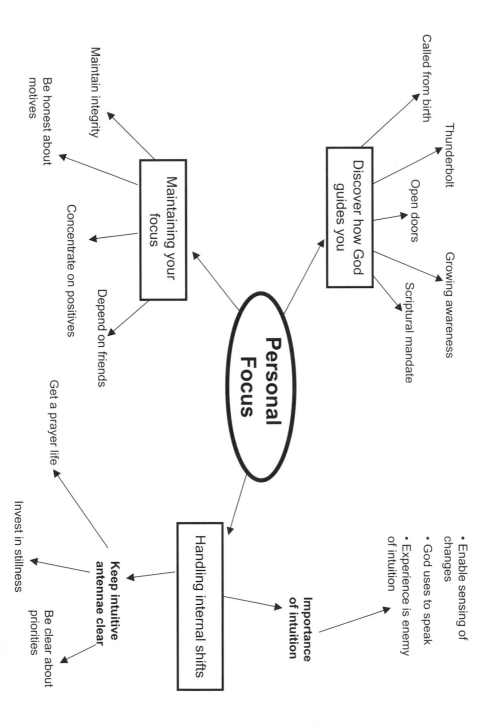

Platform Focus:
How to Communicate and Maintain Your Vision

*You can never underestimate the amount of energy and
frequency you must give to vision casting.
You can never underestimate it.*
-- Bill Hybels

Associate Pastor Susan Johnson pushed her chair away from her desk
and turned to face the window. Watching the rush-hour traffic inching
along West Street, she continued reflecting on the mixed results of the
recent congregational survey.

The influx of families from new homes and companies moving into
the area continued bringing many benefits to the once-elderly congregation. Still, while offerings were increasing and Sunday school attendance was hitting new highs, there were dark clouds hidden in the
survey's numbers and handwritten comments.

Despite the time invested in creating a vision statement, a sizeable
percentage of the congregation had little insight into the church's dis-
tinctives. Few bothered to answer survey questions about what made

this particular gathering of saints different from others. And fewer still could provide any specifics around where the church was headed.

While Associate Pastor Johnson was thankful for the new lives being touched, for the children overflowing the classrooms and the nursery, she knew there was no easy way to allay concerns over this apparent lack of information. Picking up her well-worn Bible, she began praying for wisdom for herself, for Senior Pastor Douglas, and for the board that would be discussing the vision-related results that evening.

Despite what we might like to believe, it's not our beautiful buildings, our dynamic worship, or our inspired preaching that draws people to our churches. What draws people is our vision.

Scripture makes it clear that visions are entrusted to the church's leaders. We're told, "Where there is no vision, the people perish.⁶" We're encouraged to "Write the vision and make it plain on tablets, that he may run who reads it.⁷" Without a clearly articulated vision, we might be leading people. But what's our destination?

To many of us, this isn't new information. What may be surprising, however, is the number of people in our churches who don't know, don't remember, or don't understand our vision. In his work with hundreds of churches, Dr. Chand regularly has the opportunity to see how well churches are communicating their visions. In addition to meeting with the pastor, he also meets with the first and second tiers of leadership. In each meeting, he inquires about the church's vision. Only two churches had first- and sec-

What draws people is our vision.

ond-tier leaders who precisely understood their vision.

If 90 percent of a church's leaders do not grasp the vision, it's safe to assume that the people coming to that church don't understand it either. Imagine how ineffective Wal-Mart would be if the company's vice presidents and store managers didn't comprehend their vision. Each store – and each store employee – would be figuring out what's important on their own. It would be like a shooting range where everyone had a different understanding of where the bull's-eye was located.

> Without a clearly articulated vision, we might be leading people. But what's our destination?

People need to know exactly where the center of the target is; that's exactly the information that a vision provides. It's not enough to have the vision printed in the church bulletin; the vision has to be in the hearts and minds of a church's leaders and its people. If the vision doesn't resonate with these folks, it may be because it isn't clear or succinct enough.

In addition to clearly articulating your destination and defining the target, an effective vision paints a clear picture of our desired future. According to Walt Disney, an effective vision has a way of helping to create that desired future. "The future is not the result of choices among alternate paths offered in the present. It is a place created – created first in the mind and the will; created next in activity."

Once the target is clear, it's relatively easy to see how effectively you're fulfilling that vision. The military has a term for this, known as "time on target." For many pastors, "time on target" is a problem. It's not unusual to get good proposals and suggestions about what the church should be doing. If we spend our time on every godly activity we're presented with, before long we realize that we've had little time on target, little time devoted to the vision that God has given to us.

> "The future is not the result of choices among alternate paths offered in the present. It is a place created – created first in the mind and the will; created next in activity."

To pastors and leaders who are passionate about their vision and investing themselves in this vision, discovering these gaps may be frustrating. But facing this news is also the beginning of an important change. You're now ready to effectively communicate your vision.

In this chapter, we'll discuss how to communicate your vision, examine the characteristics of an effective vision, learn about the challenges and benefits of private vision casting, and explain methods for refreshing and enlarging a vision.

Constructing an Effective Vision

Habakkuk 2:2 says, "Write the vision and make it plain on tablets, that he may run who reads it." This verse provides three important characteristics of an effective vision.

A vision should be:

- **Portable.** When we "write the vision," we want to make it easy for people to carry. If we've done this job well, anyone in the congregation should be able to clearly communicate and explain the vision to someone else.

- **Memorable.** A "plain" vision is one that's not complicated. Keeping it simple makes it easy to understand and easy to recall. You can also make it memorable by keeping it short. Ideally, it should be short enough to fit easily on a t-shirt. If it doesn't fit, it's too long, which keeps it from being memorable. Dr. Chand frequently recommends that churches link a vision to action words or spell it out using an acronym to make it more memorable.
- **Motivational.** A vision should be inspiring; it should make people want to "run with it." If no one is excited about it, it's not effective.

Here are examples of visions that fit these characteristics:

Building the House – Advancing the Kingdom

Embrace Life – Live Life – Give Life

Jump – Grow -- Soar

Experience Expansion

SWIFT	**S**pirit-Filled
	Worship Center
	International
	Family-Oriented
	Training God's People
REAL	**R**estoring Hope
	Empowering People
	Advancing the Kingdom
	Leaving a Legacy
LEAPING	**L**eading
	Evangelizing
	Assimilating
	Proclaiming
	Incarnating
	Nurturing
	Growing

Creative expressions, including artwork and illustrations can enhance a vision. The "LEAPING" vision might include an illustration of someone jumping exuberantly. Others could include drawings of helping hands or people to make them more memorable. In churches with talented musicians, it's not unusual to find a jingle communicating the vision in toe-tapping style.

The Process of Communicating a Vision

When Dr. Chand consults with a pastor who is ready to begin communicating a vision, he recommends presenting it in a phased approach, known as "deep seeding."

He begins by drawing a pyramid and dividing it into tiers to represent the various audiences within the church. The numbers of tiers vary, depending on the composition of the church.

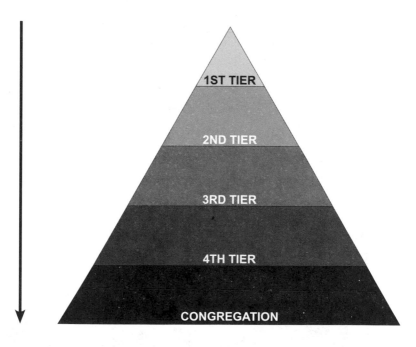

The pastor selects a day – usually a Saturday – to begin vision casting and follows these principles:

- The vision is first explained to the group in the top tier.
- Each subsequent meeting builds on the previous meeting, with the group from the first tier attending the meeting with the second tier; the first and second tiers attending the meeting with the third tier, and so on.
- In each meeting, the pastor tells each group why it's important that he talk about the vision with them and affirms the work they've done thus far.
- Any examples used must be relevant to the group being addressed.
- Each meeting has "take-away" time, where the participants are asked to communicate one primary message they obtained during the meeting. Having people articulate what they've heard reinforces the message and helps them commit to it.
- If time permits, allow for questions.
- Don't close with the question time. Reserve three to five minutes for a closing statement.

Deep seeding enables the vision to settle with one tier before communicating it to the next tier. If the previous tier doesn't understand the vision, corrections can be made before presenting it to the next group. It provides a deliberate process for taking a church through a vision.

When moving through the deep-seeding process, be sure to focus on the "what" and the "why" of the vision, rather than being distracted by the "how" and "when." Because most people are concrete thinkers, they tend to jump ahead to the "how" and "when" questions of implementation before they fully understand the "what" and the "why." You'll know this is happening when you hear questions like, "Who is going to do this," "How much will it cost," or "When is that going to get done?" Those are all very good questions but they're not questions that need to be the emphasis right now. Keep bringing the conversation back to what's being done and why it's being done. It's important to understand the difference between those questions. Focusing on the essential questions will enable us to gain people's minds and wills before asking for their committed actions and activity.

As part of the deep-seeding process, it's vital to plan a sermon series on the vision. For example, let's say the vision is "connecting people to God, to people and to purpose." In this case, there would be a five-part series that would begin with an overview, separate sermons about each of the three connections, and a sermon recapping the vision. Each sermon builds the excitement about the vision to a crescendo. The final Sunday becomes a celebratory time, where the jingle is presented and the entire congregation walks out of the church wearing identical t-shirts sporting the components of the vision on both the front and the back.

> "You can never underestimate the amount of energy and frequency you must give to vision casting."

Communication Fundamentals

Communication is more art than science, which means that there's no single right way to communicate a vision. What works best depends on your audience and the context of your situation.

However, keeping the following principles in mind will help to successfully communicate your vision in most situations:

- Take your time.
- Be intentional.
- Engage formal and informal assistants.
- Measure success in degrees.

- *Take your time.* *Vision casting* is a term that's often used to describe the process of communicating a vision. The presence of the word *cast* in this term suggests a useful fishing metaphor.

Unless you're an extremely talented or an extremely lucky fisherman, you're going to cast your line many times before you catch something. Like fishing, vision casting takes time. It's not a process that you can rush. You just have to relax and enjoy it.

Vision casting takes time. Relax and enjoy it.

As leaders, we should heed the wise advice of Bill Hybels, who said, "You can never underestimate the amount of energy and frequency you must give to vision casting. "

Too many times, we forget how long it has taken for our own vision to evolve. We don't remember the journey that God took us through to birth this vision in our hearts. All we see is the vision that burns within us. We might become impatient with others when they don't grasp it quickly or when they're easily distracted. It's not enough to hold a couple of staff meetings, preach a series, and think that the journey is completed. Vision casting takes time. Relax and enjoy it.

- *Be intentional.* It's important that you strategically and purposefully communicate your vision. Find ways to make it visible and concrete. Any time someone comes close to hitting the target, be sure to celebrate that milestone. Doing that helps people to formulate a picture of success.

Dr. Brooks' church intentionally uses various methods and media to make their vision clear. It's not unusual for him to stand up at the pulpit and say, "I want to thank Joe and Sally because here's what they did last week." He's found that people are always astounded when a pastor praises individuals from the pulpit; it's something they remember. At other times, they show a short, two-minute video of a success story on Sunday morning. And they also use printed material and their Web site to show people what a win looks like. Together, these announcements, testimonies and stories paint a more complete picture of the vision.

...helps people to formulate a picture of success.

When you're first starting out, you may not have many stories to tell. Just remember that when you don't have fire, it's okay to blow smoke. If you're close to reaching a goal – or even just launching your efforts – find ways to celebrate and announce your progress. Make it a big deal. Intentionally communicating about your strategic activities will help everyone to catch the vision.

- *Engage formal and informal assistants.* If you want your vision communicated effectively, it's also essential that you get help from two groups of people: formal and informal vision casters.

> It's also essential that you get help from two groups of people: formal and informal vision casters.

Formal vision casters are primarily your leaders and staff, together with the heads of the church's various ministries. Much of your time will be spent formally communicating the vision to these key leaders.

If these leaders have their own staffs, hold them responsible for ensuring that they communicate the vision to them. As the senior pastor, Dr. Brooks views communicating and explaining the vision as his top priority. His staff understands that he will periodically test their people's understanding of the vision. He may verbally ask a church employee to explain the vision or he might ask them to write it down. If an employee can't communicate at least some of the relevant concepts without any coaching, he challenges his staff to continue talking with their people.

Don't think that just *talking* about the vision is sufficient. In many ways, vision is like leadership; it's caught more than taught. Ultimately, it's their proximity to you that will help these leaders to catch the vision. As they see you live and

> In many ways, vision is like leadership; it's caught more than taught.

breathe the vision, it will be easier for them to catch it.

Informal vision casters are the people who tell others how their kids got saved, how a husband found camaraderie and collegiality, or how a mom finally found a group of women she can relate with.

These folks get caught up in the stories, not the verbiage, and they enthusiastically share what they see, hear and experience with others. Every time you tell these stories or praise people from the pulpit, you're targeting these folks.

When they consistently see and hear the vision, they'll start telling others and become informal vision casters. That's precisely what you want them to do!

Most church attendees won't relate to the terms of the vision explained in the bulletin. But when you start telling a story or they hear how someone's life has been touched, they can relate to that. When they consistently see and hear the

The Power of Stories

Jesus used parables to teach eternal truths. In the same way, you can use everyday stories as powerful tools to help folks catch the church's vision.

- *Remember, not everyone relates well to a written vision statement.*
- *Look for the events in people's lives that paint living examples of your vision.*
- *Find ways to communicate these examples in prominent ways.*
- *Be consistent about telling stories of how lives are touched and changed.*

vision, they'll start telling others and become informal vision casters. That's precisely what you want them to do! When "sneezers" catch the vision-virus, they sneeze on everyone contagiously. It is this story-telling sneezer that becomes the infectious vision carrier. Pray for a vision virus to break out.

• *Measure success in degrees.* If you were charged with measuring how effective another church was in communicating their vision, what would you look for?

As a starting point, you might see how prominent they've made their vision statement. You'd look to see if it's in the church bulletin or if it's hanging on the wall. If you were a good investigator, you'd also survey members as they were leaving a service. You could tell from the answers of people who've attended for a few years whether that church was doing a good job of communicating their vision.

Just because a large percentage of our folks understand the vision, we can't be tempted to think the job is over. As a church grows, it's important to ensure that new people understand and buy into the vision. If people can't do that at some level, the majority of the time, it means we have to improve our communications efforts. Or, it might be a signal that there's trouble brewing.

It's been our experience that one measure of a healthy church is the clarity of its vision. The clearer a church's vision, the less likely they are to experience a split. Most church fights are battles over who's going to control the vision. Someone has to be in control of the church's vision. If the senior pastor doesn't define and control it, someone else will try to. Continually communicating the vision, together with finding ways to gauge how well people are receiving it, are critical components of building a healthy church.

But the real success of the church is not measured by its ability to avoid a split, and it goes beyond the percentage of members engaged with the vision. All of that is great. However, the real measure of success is achieved when people who don't go to your church know what your vision is. That's when you've created a brand in your community.

> As a church grows, it's important to ensure that new people understand and buy into the vision.

We're all familiar with brands. We don't have to eat at McDonald's to know what a Happy Meal is. We don't have to shop at Sam's Club to know they're about large quantities at lower prices. We don't have to use a Dell computer to understand that they're about quality PCs. Those companies have branded themselves.

The early church was branded. In Acts 2, we know that the believers sold their possessions so they could share with the needy, that they worshipped together in their homes, and that "they enjoyed the goodwill of all the people.[8]" Even those in Jerusalem who were not believers knew something about the vision of the early church.

When you have so saturated your community that people know your vision, when they know your target, that's when you're _____ successful. You're no longer casting your vision; you've created a brand. It's also the reason that there are mul-

> The clearer a church's vision, the less likely they are to experience a split.

tiple churches; each one has a different brand. One church may have a vision for strong marriages, another may minister to certain age groups, while another focuses on some other area.

After 24 years in their community, people are recognizing Dr. Brooks' church – Grace Outreach Center, Plano, TX -- for their vision for children's ministries. One of the area magazines voted them the number-one children's ministry in the county. Even though no one from the church was part of the survey, people in the community knew what their vision was.

Challenges & Benefits of Private Vision Casting

In addition to publicly communicating your vision, it's also necessary to privately communicate the church's vision to select individuals and small groups. In most cases, this private vision casting is done either with believers who are highly influential or who have a high net-worth.

It's understandable why we might want to avoid these private meetings. Perhaps our audience's influence or income makes us feel awkward. Or perhaps we have the type of leadership gift where we're only comfortable before a crowd. While those feelings are understandable, we simply cannot avoid scheduling private meetings where we can personally share our vision.

Let's say you're trying to raise funds for a capital expansion. You might want to build a Christian school, a youth center, or start some other worthy project. When you talk about this campaign from the pulpit, you're speaking to the 80 percent of the congregation that are typically not equipped to make sizeable contributions. The majority of your donations will come from privately sharing your vision with that smaller percentage of believers who have the time, the talent, or the treasure to move that vision forward. Getting these influential and high net-worth believers on your team is simply the best use of your time. It's the 80-20 rule at work.

> The real measure of success is achieved when people who don't go to your church know what your vision is.

Once we've overcome that initial hesitation at meeting with these folks, we'll need to begin gathering some information. We'll have to:

1. Identify the influencers
2. Learn their language
3. Discern what's important to them

1. Identify the influencers. If we don't know who's part of that vital 20 percent, we have to begin identifying them. That means finding out who it is that influences other people, as well as those who can influence the project through their giving.

There are various creative ways to accomplish this. It might involve identifying the folks in the later stages of their lives who enjoy a good reputation in your community. It also involves identifying your biggest financial contributors. When John Maxwell was pastoring, for example, he made a point of having lunch with people who consistently put a thousand dollars or more in the offering.

> In addition to publicly communicating your vision, it's also necessary to privately communicate the church's vision to select individuals and small groups.

2. Learn their language. People don't all speak the same language. Some are more captivated by launching a project, while others are captivated by its potential.

- With the people captivated by a project, we can describe the short-term challenges of getting the project started.
- With those more interested in the potential, we can tell them about the effect it will have on people, how it will enable us to provide instruction, or the results we hope to produce.

3. **Discern what's important to them.** Many people want to make a difference for God's kingdom. By supplying concrete actions for the influencers we've identified, we can help them to see these desires fulfilled.

For example, youth ministry is the heart of Dr. Brooks' church. When he meets with influencers, he helps them to see that it's not necessary for everyone to be a Sunday school teacher or a youth worker. They can participate in this ministry just by employing the gifts God has given them. With some, he's able to make the contribution personally hit home. If he knows how fervently a man is praying for a grandchild's salvation, he might remind him that the project will help someone else's grandchild. In the end, the conversation shows each person how they'll be helping to change lives for eternity.

Whether you meet with influencers individually or in groups depends on the size of your church and the anticipated group dynamics.

- In large churches, there may be advantages to having individual meetings. At Dr. Brooks' church – which has an attendance of 4,500 – he finds that he gets better results and raises more funds from individual meetings.
- One disadvantage of group meetings is that it's more difficult to create or maintain a successful environment. Someone who has a high level of doubt or a lot of questions can magnify whatever doubt is already in the room. This person might not be trying to be negative; they could just be focusing on details when you're speaking in broad terms. But it can be harder to control the mood.

> One disadvantage of group meetings is that it's more difficult to create or maintain a successful environment.

- Individual meetings also enable people to ask you questions that they might not ask publicly. And these meetings provide an influencer with your full attention without the risk of the conversation being sidetracked.
- Some combination of group and individual meetings can also be effective. For example, once the

influencers are identified, we can divide them into three groups: the top ten percent, the next forty, and the bottom fifty. The top ten percent and their spouses are invited to the pastor's house for dinner. There, the vision is cast and everyone

> ...the best solution may require stepping out of our comfort zones.

is asked to pray about their involvement. The follow up can be conducted at subsequent individual meetings. And the process can continue – with or without dinner – for the other two groups.

It's important to consider the church culture before deciding on how to approach this method of vision casting. It's too easy to decide to speak to groups because that plays to the strength of a pastor. Many of us are simply more comfortable addressing groups. In the end, the best solution may require stepping out of our comfort zones.

We should develop whatever skills we need to cast our vision individually. The biggest reason for the one-on-one approach is simple: it's the way that influencers are used to being addressed. It's what they expect. Because of that, it's a way for us to develop credibility and ask them to pray about being involved.

Once the influencers are identified, involved, and the project is under way, find ways to encourage them by making the vision tangible. Grace Outreach Center designed a service that let the congregation see and hear about the many lives affected by its growing children's ministry. After the service, Dr. Brooks individually approached the influencers who were there, putting his arm around them and said, "Thank you. Without you, this never could have happened."

It was a powerful way to keep these folks connected to the on-going vision of the church.

Refreshing and Enlarging a Vision

Visions are never cast in concrete. They're living, breathing reflections of an approaching destiny. As we near that destiny, it's only natural that our vision will grow, expand and change.

Acts 9 describes the encounter on the road to Damascus that launched Paul's ministry. In Acts 26 and 27, he describes new levels of understanding about the same vision. The further Paul walked in his vision, the clearer it became.

The core, the essence, and the fundamentals of a vision will always remain the same. Over time, what changes are the ways the vision is implemented. In addition, as the people responding to the vision change, so do the dynamics of that vision.

In the 25 years since Grace Outreach Center was founded, their vision for youth and children's ministries expanded as the surrounding community grew. In the beginning, it was relatively easy to cast a vision for a children's ministry to parents with a corresponding need. Later, the vision shifted, as the church began drawing people who simply believed in the value of Jesus' mandate to "suffer the little ones to come unto Me." Then, the vision enlarged again as it began to appeal to those who didn't have children, who simply witnessed its power.

> The biggest reason for the one-on-one approach is simple: it's the way that influencers are used to being addressed.

While this last group wasn't necessarily the target audience, just being around youth ministered to them.

The church's demographics have also changed drastically. The adults who were its early members became grandparents, and the children they sent to children's church became adults with children of their own. Today, Grace finds itself with five generations of believers in its congregation. Like many churches, it's being challenged to keep its vision relevant for a changing demographic.

> Visions are never cast in concrete. They're living, breathing reflections of an approaching destiny.

In the process, they've learned again the importance of clearly and intentionally telling the story of the vision. During one service, hundreds of those affected by the children's ministry – from six to 36 years old – stood on stage. As each preschooler, college student, and parent gave their name and described how they were saved in children's church, the power of the vision grew clearer and clearer. The vision was no longer words; it was faces, it was lives, it was people.

Despite changing demographics, a vision can still be the mortar that holds everything together. Grace Outreach Center links every ministry to its focus on youth. Both the men's and women's ministries aim at developing the godly people who will raise godly children. And the senior's center regularly gets visits from the children's choir and the drama team. By continually focusing on how to link its ministries to its core vision, the church avoids having five generations fighting for time, for

> The further Paul walked in his vision, the clearer it became.

talent and for a share of its treasury. Instead, the vision becomes the cement that joins them together.

Strategic Planning for a Vision

Transforming a vision into reality means ensuring that every aspect of the vision is implemented throughout the organization. This requires:

- Strategic planning
- Vision-centric evaluation

Strategic Planning. Effective planning means answering many questions about how a vision will be implemented. This can be accomplished with a planning grid similar to this one.

What	Why	Who	How	When	Where	How Much	Accountable to Whom	Evaluation Process

Successful implementation is dependent on developing a corresponding plan for each point within the vision, a plan that describes all the related components and actions.

Following this detailed planning process produces a plan that is *workable* and *measurable*. Developing these specifics also produces *buy in* within the organization from the plan's built-in *accountability* and its ability to develop a *transparent* organization.

Vision-Centric Evaluation. Successfully implementing a

vision also requires a thorough evaluation, which ensures that everything in the organization is vision centric. Everything that's done has to be connected to the vision. Anything that's not connected to the vision needs to justify its continued existence.

One way to accomplish this evaluation is to have every department in the church categorize everything they do under a component of the vision. If the vision is LEAP – Leading, Evangelizing, Assimilating and Proclaiming – all programs and activities should fit into one of the first four columns in the following chart. If something doesn't fit, it's put into the fifth column – NOT US.

> The vision was no longer words; it was faces, it was lives, it was people.

NAME OF DEPARTMENT:				
NAME OF LEADER:				
L	E	A	P	NOT US

After the pastor receives this evaluation from the various department heads, it's time to begin evaluating the items placed in the last column. If there's sufficient justification, programs that are not connected to the vision can be:

- Continued
- Phased out over time
- Immediately discontinued

When all the evaluations are completed, that's when a general plan for the organization emerges, a plan that's completely vision centric. With this plan, it's time to begin discussing:

- Programs
- Personnel and staffing
- Budget allocation
- Facility usage
- Resources
- Scheduling
- Special events
- Guest speakers
- Conferences
- Retreats
- And more

Everything that happens within the organization must be evaluated through the lens provided by the vision. Once everything is justified by its connection to the vision, it creates an organization that is laser focused. That focus comes from having a vision that is embedded in the organizational DNA. It results in leaders seeing how their trans-dependency requires dedicated teamwork. All of this work creates an organization that is branded.

Implementing a vision in this fashion produces an organization that is:

- Synergized – Having several components and entities merged into seamless cooperation
- Galvanized – Composed of different elements knit into a unified whole
- Energized – Filled with a creative sense of excitement and direction

That's the type of organization that attracts people, attracts capable leaders, and produces fruit for God's kingdom – fruit that remains[9].

Teaching Points

- Scripture makes it clear that visions are entrusted to church leaders.
- People need to know exactly where the center of the target is, which is what a vision provides.
- A vision should be:
  - Portable. Easy for others to communicate and explain.
  - Memorable. Simple, easy to understand and easy to recall.
  - Motivational. Inspiring.
- Communicating a vision in a phased approach is known as "deep seeding."
  - Divide the church into tiers representing its various audiences.
  - Everyone from the previous tier attends the presentation to the next tier.
  - Focus on the "what" and the "why" of the vision, rather than being distracted by the "how" and "when."
  - It's vital to plan a sermon series on the vision.
- There's no single right way to communicate a vision. What works best depends on your audience and the context of your situation
  - Take your time. Too often, we forget how long it has taken for our own vision to evolve.
  - Be intentional. Strategically and purposefully communicate your vision. Find ways to make it visible and concrete.

- Engage formal and informal assistants. Get help from formal and informal vision casters.
- Measure success in degrees. Continually communicate the vision and find ways to gauge how well people are receiving it.
- It's necessary to privately communicate to select individuals and small groups.
  - In most cases, this is done either with highly influential or high net-worth believers.
  - Private vision casting involves:
    - Identifying the influencers. Finding out who influences others, as well as those who can influence through their giving.
    - Learn their language. Some are attracted by project potential; others want to overcome short-term challenges.
    - Discern what's important to them. Many want to make a difference for God's kingdom. Supply them with concrete actions.
  - Whether you meet with influencers individually or in groups depends on the size of the church and group dynamics.
- Visions are living, breathing reflections of an approaching destiny that will grow, expand and change.
  - The core and fundamentals of a vision always remain the same.
  - What changes over time are the ways a vision is implemented.
  - Despite changing demographics, a vision can be the mortar that holds a church together.

- Strategic planning ensures that a vision is implemented throughout an organization.
    - It involves developing a corresponding plan for each point in the vision.
    - A vision-centric evaluation ensures that everything is connected to the vision.
    - Programs not connected can be continued, phased out, or immediately stopped.
    - When everything is justified by the vision, it produces an organization that is laser focused.

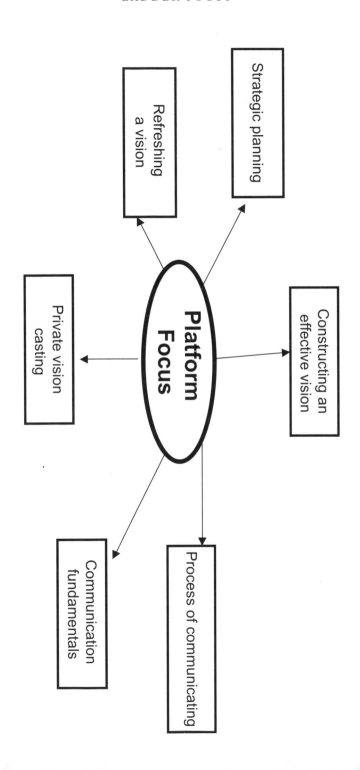

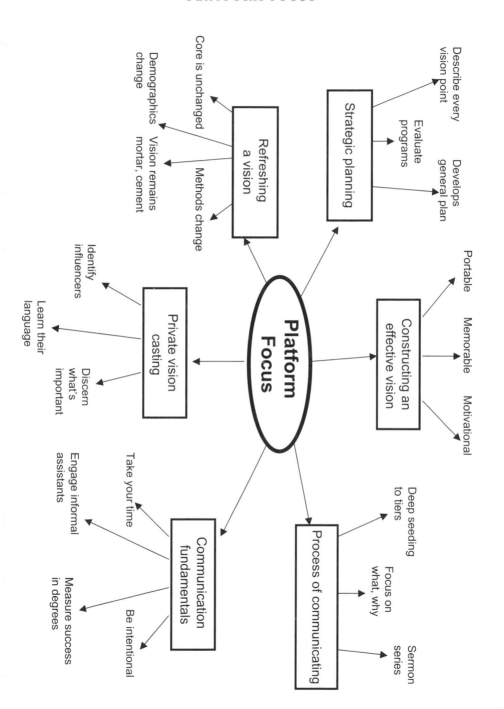

3

People Focus: How to Develop Leaders

*Every leader is capable of building his or her own
kingdom dream team...Through the power of the Holy Spirit,
the ability to build such a team is a standard component
in every leader's gift package.*
-- *Courageous Leadership* by Bill Hybels

*When you attract a follower, you add to the church.
When you develop a leader, you multiply the church.*
-- John Maxwell

A room filled with laughing teenagers, an unfinished sermon, and the final details for tomorrow morning's men's prayer breakfast. Like tag-team wrestlers, these three events took turns keeping Pastor Jake Barrett's mind fully occupied during every minute of a rainy Friday afternoon.

As evening arrived, the door of the multi-purpose room began opening and shutting punctuating the arrival of each youth group attendee. Since the departure of his youth pastor, Jake was the only one available to tend to this gathering. He'd spent a few hours with a borrowed guitar that afternoon, trying to learn a few worship songs, but he wisely dismissed that idea in favor of an acappella approach.

Pushing his sermon notes aside, Jake made two unsuccessful calls to confirm food deliveries for tomorrow's breakfast. While waiting on hold, he began modifying the advertisement he'd used to hire his last youth pastor. At the instant that his wife opened his door to signal him to start the meeting, a loud dial tone echoed through the receiver. Realizing that the deli had disconnected him again, Jake dropped the want ad, hung up the phone and headed toward the waiting youth group.

If we wanted to discover a senior pastor's philosophy of ministry, the best approach might be to observe how he or she approaches operating a church.

Typically, senior church leaders rely on one of three strategies for accomplishing the work of the ministry:

1. *Do-it-yourself.* While this method only seems practical in smaller churches, it also appeals to leaders who need a sense of control. The downside is obvious -- it can be an awful lot of work.
3. *Hire help.* Bringing in leaders can create a ministry team, but it means paying salaries and providing benefits. It can be a costly endeavor.
4. *Develop people.* Growing your own leaders requires a large investment of time. It also offers many advantages.

If our churches are going to last, it's imperative that we develop people into the leaders we need. Raising up leaders is a more effective way to minister and a more efficient use of our resources. But development only occurs when you realize that other people can bring the ministry to a place you could never reach alone.

Do-it-yourself – Too much work.
Hire it out – Too much money.
Develop leaders – Too much time.

In this chapter, we'll examine some of the reasons that leaders are not being developed, we'll examine some important characteristics of development, and we'll look at different types of leaders and examine development principles.

Why Churches Don't Develop Leaders

The majority of leaders are busy doing it themselves, busy hiring or they're just plain busy. While more of today's leaders are developing others, this method still isn't on the radar of a sufficient number of churches.

There are a number of reasons for not developing leaders:

- Pressing demands
- Past disappointment
- Fear of vulnerability
- Repeating a pattern

Pressing demands. Many leaders feel pulled in different directions. We're trying to cast our vision, we have sermons to develop and preach, we're attempting to raise funds for the ministry, and we're trying to draft responsible people to take

> ...we've let the good become the enemy of the best.

on other duties. Innately, we know that developing leaders takes time, which is always in such short supply. If we have trouble saying no, time is an even more valuable commodity.

When the press of daily responsibilities and the urgency of the moment keep us from developing leaders, we've let the good become the enemy of the best.

Past disappointment. Scripture illustrates how disappointment might keep us from developing other leaders. When

> The key to mentoring others is to let them see your heart.

Moses was on Mt. Sinai receiving the Ten Commandments, Aaron was down below overseeing Israel's wild fraternity party. When Moses returned, he found that the leader he trusted had seriously blown it.

When we raise up leaders, there will always be those that disappoint us. Often, it's the leaders we spend the most time with who can cause us the greatest hurt. And because we've been hurt, we may not continue developing leaders.

If we aren't willing to encounter an Aaron who might disappoint us, we will never find the Joshua who will carry on after us.

Fear of vulnerability. The key to mentoring others is to let them see your heart. If we're going to develop high-level leaders, we've got to let them get close enough to us for that to happen.

For some of us, exposing our heart seems a dangerous thing.

> We have to be willing to pour our heart into someone else. We have to be willing to take a risk. The key to mentoring others is to let them see your heart.

That's why people pay counselors and consultants; because they need a safe place to show their heart. When we're developing a leader, we can't just put our best foot forward; we have to be able to reveal our doubts and our fears too. We have to be willing to pour our heart into someone else. We have to be willing to take a risk.

Repeating a pattern. Once certain patterns of behavior are ingrained in people, they're difficult to break. These patterns can range from harmless but annoying habits to more serious ones. For example, children who grow up in dysfunctional homes tend to continue the bad habits they learned there. In the same way, pastors who were never mentored continue the learned pattern of not developing other leaders.

Dr. Chand's Experience

I was raised in a pastor's home in India, graduated from Bible College, went to seminary, and rose from pastoring to being the district overseer of churches in Indiana, Wisconsin, Illinois and Michigan. Despite those blessings, I can't recall a mentor approaching me and showing an interest in my development. No one approached me and said, "I see some God-given gifts in you. Let me put my arm around you and help and guide you. Here's my phone number, here's my e-mail address. Call me, write me, let me help you."

When I realized this lack and saw its effect, I grew disappointed and angry. I wondered why people with foresight didn't direct me around problems they might have seen coming my way. But this thinking came to a sudden stop when I realized something important: the leaders around me did not develop *me* because nobody had developed *them*. Instead of being a stumbling block, that realization became the motivation that drives my passion for leadership development. It's my way of helping other leaders to break the pattern.

If no one mentored or developed us, we won't have a model for development. Typically, we'll only teach in the way in which we were taught and we'll only give away what we have. We simply cannot pass on what we don't possess.

Once we realize that, we have to look for ways to break that cycle. We can begin to seek out mentors and find people that will speak in our lives. Finding a mentor is not as difficult as it might sound. When you're shopping for a mentor, look for someone who has goals that are similar to yours, who is doing what you'd like to do, or who has gifts you'd like to possess. If you're able to, you can also hire a coach to provide some specific or specialized development.

> We simply cannot pass on what we don't possess.

Not all development has to come from these formal mentoring relationships. There are many informal mentors who can mentor us for years through their CDs and books. When you're listening and reading, be sure that you're asking the right questions. If we ask "what" questions, all we get is information. If we ask "why" questions, we can discover the principles that provide the foundations to understanding. Asking the right questions is the key.

Dr. Chand's Perspective

A mentoring relationship should help us to develop the ability to think differently, to think like a leader. One of my friends once had an opportunity to spend a few hours with Bishop Eddie Long. Wanting to make the most of this time, my friend e-mailed me asking for advice about the kinds of

> questions he should ask Bishop Long.
>
> I encouraged him not to focus on questions. Instead, I advised him to just have a casual conversation and try to discover how Bishop Long thinks. By figuring out how he reaches his conclusions, how he makes his decisions, how he implements strategies, my friend would be training himself to think like his mentor.

When we realize that we haven't been mentored, we cannot afford to linger in our disappointment. We can't afford to let the next generation of leaders learn the hard way, the way that we learned. We have to take responsibility for the next generation and do the right thing for the Kingdom. We have to pass on the blessing of mentoring to the next generation of leaders and enable them to move on ahead of us.

> If we ask "what" questions, all we get is information. If we ask "why" questions, we can discover the principles that provide the foundations to understanding. Asking the right questions is the key.

Development Assessment

Answering these four questions will help you to develop your own action plan for leadership development.

- Do you let others participate in the ministry instead of doing it all yourself?

- Do you have a consuming passion to develop the church's next generation of leaders? If not, what can you do to get started?

> - Have you begun targeting people into whom you can pour your time and energy?
>
> - Are you releasing people into ministry, enabling them to grow and fail without fear?

The Critical Difference: Training vs. Developing

Many pastors make a common mistake. They think they're developing another leader – or even being developed themselves – when they're only being trained for a job.

It's vital that we understand these fundamental differences between training and developing:

- **Training focuses on tasks and is less risky.** We train people all the time. We train ushers, children's workers, and greeters. Then we place them in this fixed role within a certain environment. They have constrictions around them, they have do's and don'ts, and they usually have a supervisor. If they do make mistakes, they're usually not anything of a high-stakes nature.

> If a person is really developed by you, they'll be able to finish your sentences. They'll know how you think.

- **Development focuses on people, not on tasks.** Development aims much higher than ensuring that someone can perform a job. And because development is *people focused* rather than *task focused*, it requires giving *yourself*. If a person is really developed by you, they'll be able to finish your sentences. They'll know how you think. They'll know how you approach conflict resolution, how you develop solutions and how you carry out initiatives. In the process of developing a leader, you pass on part of yourself.

- **We should develop people first, and then train those we've developed.** Some pastors want to train people, see who is faithful and then develop only those people. We want people to prove themselves before we're willing to give them any time. Unfortunately, this can result in people feeling used. We should always put the person ahead of what they can do. Otherwise, we're going to have people that do the right things and have underdeveloped character, questionable motives, or poor attitudes.

> In the process of developing a leader, you pass on part of yourself.

- **Once someone is developed, they can be trained for a number of tasks.** We can cross-reference those we've developed so that they can be Sunday school teachers, ushers, and fill a number of other roles. But this is only possible *after* they're developed.

- **In training, we give people jobs. In development, we give people responsibility.** Training someone to teach children is a job; but giving them the challenge of nurturing, growing and guiding children is development.

It often takes great disappointment to bring us new understanding. Dr. Chand learned the important distinction between training and developing in this fashion.

Dr. Chand's Experience

After hearing that a church that I pastored for nine years had been through five pastors and two splits since I relocated in 1989, I began analyzing how my actions might have contributed. As I looked back, I concluded that I did a great job of raising followers. However, I did an abysmal job -- if any at all -- of developing leaders.

I concluded that it was because I provided great training but didn't do any developing. If I had invested my time in developing leaders, if I had poured my heart into them so they could finish my sentences, carry out the vision, and mentor another generation of leaders, perhaps these difficulties could have been avoided.

While I'll never know for certain, I wonder.

Developing the Four Types of Leaders

In training, one size fits all. We can train all of our ushers, our greeters and our Sunday school teachers to perform the same tasks in the same way.

Development however, requires a more tailored approach.

More churches are beginning to borrow from the business-oriented human resources model. They're considering personality types and employing style inventories to find the most efficient way to develop people. Willow Creek is

> We should always put the person ahead of what they can do.

just one example of this; they identify a person's talents and then provide the training and development that suits them.

The business model helps us to avoid a common problem in leadership development: a tendency to develop people past the point where they need to be developed. Churches often take someone with a specific ability and try to get him or her to also become good at additional skills that are not part of their abilities. We tell them, "You are a leader. It's great that you're good at X; now here are Y and Z." That type of thinking can get us into trouble. The development that we provide has to be appropriate.

> It often takes great disappointment to bring us new understanding.

Identifying the Four Leadership Types

There are many useful methods of classifying leaders that can help us to determine how to best develop them. Let's examine these four categories (PEAS) of leadership types:

- Positional
- Entrepreneurial
- Administrative
- Spiritual

Type of Leader	Developmental Need
Positional Leader	Give a job
Entrepreneurial Leader	Give understanding
Administrative Leader	Give trust
Spiritual Leader	Give opportunity

Positional leaders have very specific skills. They might be good at organization, or accounting. We may have to invest some time in helping them to discover this strength so they can apply this talent. Sometimes, a talent will be readily apparent to you or to them. And sometimes, a leader may see a specific talent but may not think that there's a way to apply it within the church. Once a positional leader's talent is discovered, you can focus on providing whatever training is needed to apply their gift.

Entrepreneurial leaders have a pioneer spirit combined with an astute business sense. The right entrepreneurial leader can come alongside a senior pastor and find creative ways to leverage the church's economic assets. In the process, they're going to help to discover new opportunities and extend the ministry. The right entrepreneurial leader can be a blessing to the pastor who's ready to admit their need in the area of business. If we're going to bring on an entrepreneurial leader, we have to be willing to trust them. It's not necessary to completely understand everything they're doing, but they have to be trusted. And we're going to have to trust them at a higher level than we trust the other three types of leaders.

> The business model helps us to avoid a common problem in leadership development: a tendency to develop people past the point where they need to be developed.

Administrative leaders have the ability to connect A and B. Their management focus means that there's less of a need for training and more of a need for them to simply understand your organization. You should give them a behind-the-scenes tour of the church that God wants you to build and manage. Show them how things are inter-related, what's good and what needs improvement. It's not a case of a clear-cut task; these leaders need trust before they can make the improvements that they're equipped to see and to implement.

Some pastors are somewhat unwilling to give up these endeavors. They'll readily tell us, "I'm no good at business." When we recommend that they get someone around them with a good business sense, they hesitate. "I've heard that if you don't control the money, you don't control the ministry," they'll say. We always remind them that people who are no good at business and who control the money are likely to find themselves with no money to control. After that, some of them finally relent.

Spiritual leaders are those who are wired for spirituality. These are the leaders mentioned in Acts 6, the ones who know they should be devoting themselves to the Word and to prayer. With these leaders, we provide them with an environment in which they can exercise this gift. It doesn't necessarily mean preaching from the pulpit; it might involve leading corporate prayer, worship, or Bible study.

> ...people who are no good at business and who control the money are likely to find themselves with no money to control.

Developing the Four Leadership Types

Have you ever been in a car designed to run on premium fuel that was operating on regular gas? The results aren't worth the few pennies in savings. Cars that need high-octane gas complain audibly and perform poorly when they don't get the right fuel. The engine knocks, sometimes it smokes, it's just not pretty.

Likewise, each of the four leadership styles is designed with particular needs. Because each has a different gift, we can't provide them with the same development path and expect them to perform well. We can't expect an entrepreneur to thrive if provided with the identical development input given to an administrative leader. Their needs are different.

As the following chart illustrates, each leadership type has a distinct operating style, different environmental considerations and their own development needs.

Type of Leader	Style	Environmental Need	Development Need
Positional	Doing	Responsibility	Job-related training
Entrepreneurial	Creating opportunity	Trust	Background in many areas
Administrative	Managing	Understanding	Knowledge of organizational operation
Spiritual	Divinely inspired	Opportunity	Quiet time

Understanding each style and adhering to these four development principles will help us to build effective leaders:

1. Know thyself.
2. Build a balanced team.
3. Honor each member.
4. Unite under a single vision.

1. Know thyself. It's important that the senior pastor distinguish his or her own style before developing other leaders. An understanding of our own style guards against the negative effects of "The Law of Affinity," which can be simply stated as "Like likes like."

Human nature has a myopic tendency to think that everyone else is just like us. Or *should be* just like us. Entrepreneurs prefer to develop everyone like they're entrepreneurs, even if those that they're developing happen to be spiritual leaders. When a spiritual leader is in charge of development, the entrepreneurial leaders on the team might be developed according to the spiritual style. Certainly, some cross-development between styles might be desirable. But if we overemphasize our style or are insensitive to the others, we're going to frustrate the very people we're trying to develop.

> "Like likes like."

2. Build a balanced team. Like likes like. An entrepreneurial leader tends to favor other entrepreneurial types. You'll hear the entrepreneurial leader saying, "Administrative people drive me crazy! They're always asking questions; they want to understand why. Forget that, let's move on."

Once we understand our own tendencies, gifts and needs, it's important that we create a balanced team. Just as churches need the five-fold ministry gifts described in Ephesians, we need to find a complementary balance among leadership styles. We need positional types to get tasks accomplished, administrators to manage our resources, entrepreneurs to create new opportunities, and spiritual leaders to discern a godly course.

> Once we understand our own tendencies, gifts and needs, it's important that we create a balanced team.

Certainly, chairing a meeting of the entire team might be challenging. But we can minimize that challenge by ensuring that everybody around the table knows why everyone is there. We have to help everyone on the team to find the balance.

Over and over again, the senior pastor has to say, "The reason Susan is here is because she's a positional leader who gets things done. We give her a job and we don't have to worry about it. It's off my list. That's why Susan is here. Jake is here because he sees opportunities when we've come to the end of the road. He's entrepreneurial. He knows how to leverage strengths that we never would have imagined and takes us to places we never considered."

> We need positional types to get tasks accomplished, administrators to manage our resources, entrepreneurs to create new opportunities, and spiritual leaders to discern a godly course.

By ensuring the entire team understands everyone's gifts, we also minimize their frustrations with each other. It reduces the tension that occurs when the entrepreneurial type wants to move forward and the spiritual person wants to pray more about a decision. Having that balance promotes understanding.

Building a balanced team also means putting the right people in the right positions. We don't want to recruit someone with an entrepreneurial style and put him in a positional slot. Neither would we expect the positional leader to create leveraged financial opportunities. As Dr. Chand's book *Who's Holding Your Ladder* says,

> ...we can minimize that challenge by ensuring that everybody around the table knows why everyone is there.

"Proper People Placement Prevents Problems."

3. *Honor each member.* It's human nature that causes us to wonder which of the four styles is more important or necessary, to think that the spiritual type is more honorable than the administrative style. Ranking the leadership styles is akin to trying to determine

> By ensuring the entire team understands everyone's gifts, we also minimize their frustrations with each other.

whether the right or left wing of an airplane is more important. We need every part to keep us balanced, hold us aloft and keep us flying.

In practical terms, we have to ensure that each leadership style is able to function according to their gifting and that everyone appreciates the diversity of styles. We'll want to ensure that not every entrepreneurial idea gets shot down, for example. We don't want anyone to feel undervalued and begin disengaging.

As Scripture tells us, every part of the human body has a necessary function. We can't have an entire body that's an eye. Neither can we have a team that's entirely positional, entrepreneurial, administrative, or spiritual. God has joined us together so that we can function together cooperatively.

4. *Unite under a single vision.* While we can appreciate different leadership styles, a church can only move forward under one vision. There can be di-versity of function, but not diversi-ty of vision. Positional leaders will function differently than entrepre-neurial leaders. Entrepreneurial

> Building a balanced team also means putting the right people in the right positions.

leaders will function differently than spiritual leaders. And spiritual leaders will function differently than administrative leaders. But all of them must function on the same grid like PEAS in a pod. There may be a certain amount of strife, tension and differences on the team. But the senior leader has to ensure that everyone operates and unites under a single vision.

Key Ingredients of Leadership Development

Every journey needs a destination. The journey of leadership development is no different. How will we know when we've arrived? Since leadership development is an on-going process, perhaps it's more appropriate to define the desired end result.

> Ranking the leadership styles is akin to trying to determine whether the right or left wing of an airplane is more important.

Leadership is *the capacity and the will to rally men and women to a common purpose.* This definition provides us with a clear picture of the type of leaders we want to produce.

In addition to having a picture of the end result, we must ensure that we know what's required during this journey. Leadership development cannot occur until we have all of the necessary ingredients. If we omit any of the following leadership development needs, the end result will suffer:

1. Vision
2. Prayer
3. A plan
4. Opportunity
5. Recognition
6. Time
7. Gratitude
8. Self-development
9. Freedom

1. *Vision.* Vision is the first item on the list for a reason: it's the air that leaders breathe. Vision is the atmosphere that ensures a leader's survival. We must provide a vision, a vision that both sustains and needs leaders.

2. *Prayer.* Jesus prayed for his disciples; we can certainly do no less. In the end, it is God working through us to develop leaders. We must pray for ourselves and for those we develop. We must pray regularly and we must pray specifically.

3. *A Plan.* While we cannot know every twist and turn along the road, we must have a general direction, a plan for developing leaders. We have to invest time and energy in thinking through the plan and understanding it intimately.

4. *Opportunity.* Those we develop cannot sit idly by. We must provide them with genuine opportunities to use their gifts. We must delegate responsibilities to them, let them learn on-the-job, trust them, and make ourselves available for on-going guidance.

5. *Recognition.* In our zeal to develop good leaders, we can forget to balance criticism with recognition. Too many times, we let our expectations and high standards stand in the way of positive comments. There's nothing that helps a developing leader to thrive more than sincere praise and recognition. Praise them regularly and praise them genuinely. Let them know how you feel about them.

> There can be diversity of function, but not diversity of vision.

Make sure that you recognize them privately but be sure to also recognize them publicly.

6. *Time.* There are no shortcuts to leadership development. We must carve time from our busy schedules and make mentoring a priority.

7. *Gratitude.* Every leader that God gives us to develop is a gift. We should be grateful for the opportunity to develop others and for the trust that God has given us.

8. *Self-development.* To develop other leaders, *we* must be growing. We should have our own personal development plan and our own mentors. In order for us to teach, we must be willing to be taught.

9. *Freedom.* Every parent knows that someday our children will leave home. There is also an appropriate time to release the leaders we've developed. That doesn't mean that the relationship ends; it only means the relationship changes. We must look toward the day when we can release healthy leaders to minister freely in the Kingdom.

To arrive at our destination, we must keep to the highway. We can't afford to take unnecessary side trips and should steer clear of dead-end avenues. Along the journey of leadership development, we must also avoid these six common leadership killers:

> There are no shortcuts to leadership development.

1. Micromanagement
2. Fearful leadership
3. Lack of resources
4. Making failure fatal
5. Creating a glass ceiling
6. Allowing end runs

1. *Micromanagement.* The "my way or the highway" attitude has no place in the development of godly leaders. We should never insist that someone only do things our way.

2. *Fearful leadership.* It's unproductive when those we're attempting to develop are afraid of our reactions or afraid to confide in us. If we're going to develop healthy leaders, we must provide them with a safe environment.

> Make sure that you recognize them privately but be sure to also recognize them publicly.

3. *Lack of resources.* If the leaders we develop are going to succeed, we must be sure that they have every resource they need.

4. *Making failure fatal.* Someone once said that we only make mistakes when we haven't learned anything from our errors. We have to ensure that we provide developing leaders with the opportunity to fail and the opportunity to learn and move on.

5. *Creating a glass ceiling.* We have to provide developing leaders with a career path. We cannot limit their potential opportunities.

6. *Allowing end runs.* Once we provide our developing leaders with responsibility, we can't allow others
to routinely ignore them or go over their heads. We
must protect them and ensure they get the respect
that they deserve.

A Leadership Development Model

Churches develop leaders in various ways. At Grace Outreach Center, the leadership development process begins
the minute someone turns the lead-
ership of his or her life over to Jesus Christ.

We must look toward the
day when we can release
healthy leaders to minister
freely in the Kingdom.

Grace has a full-time pastor who has
the job of being the initial caregiver
to all new believers. Before deciding on this approach, Dr.
Brooks looked at a number of other independent churches
that had a full-time pastor, rather than a layperson, charged
with this responsibility.

As the pastor begins caring for someone who's new in the
faith, he'll recommend the appropriate Sunday school program for that person. In this setting, a new believer begins
to understand the basics. They'll learn about exercising
faith in God and the importance of fellowship with other
believers.

At the same time that they're learning the basics, they'll begin to hear that every new creation
has a gift, a talent, or an ability that
can bring life to others. That gift
may be natural in its orientation or it may be spiritual in

In order for us to teach, we
must be willing to be taught.

its orientation. The initial-care pastor helps them to understand that natural gifts that are used spiritually can still have spiritual impact, just as spiritual gifts can have natural impact.

> If we're going to develop healthy leaders, we must provide them with a safe environment.

Even though they're in what may be their first Sunday school class, they're also experiencing their first taste of leadership development. Understandably, someone who is 20 years old gets somewhat different development from someone who is 50 years old.

In addition to helping new believers develop leadership gifts, Grace focuses on growing its leadership team. The church's leadership culture is built around six concepts, called the six Ps:

- Pastoring
- Prayer
- Placement
- Preparation
- Promotion
- Providing

Pastoring is the frontline of Grace's leadership development. Each of Dr. Brooks' direct reports is accountable for finding and nurturing new leaders, as well as for documenting this work to the board every six months.

Looking for leaders doesn't mean selectively searching for seminary graduates and MBAs within the congregation. The pastors are reminded repeatedly that few of the people they work with will look like leaders when they initially encounter them. Dr. Brooks brings this point home with an example from the life of King David. Scripture says that the

...we only make mistakes when we haven't learned anything from our errors.

people that God sent to David were stressed, depressed, and poor[10]. Many of these same people grew to become his mighty men of valor. Emphasizing the skill of pastoring in this way develops a particular type of leader, one who has witnessed first-hand the importance of pastoral care.

Prayer provides a firm foundation for all leadership development. The church takes seriously Jesus' charge in Matt. 9:37-38, "The harvest is plentiful but the laborers are few, pray therefore..." For Grace, praying for laborers is synonymous with praying for leaders. Those prayers involve two things:

- Praying that God gives wisdom, strength and enhanced abilities to the leaders they currently have
- The ability to recognize new leaders as God sends them

Placement of a leader is viewed as critically important. The

We must protect them and ensure they get the respect that they deserve.

church recognizes that the quickest way to lose a leader is to have them in the wrong position. It doesn't matter how great their leadership potential is or how big their heart is. Improper placement always leads to problems.

Grace spends a lot of time listening while their new leaders talk. They encourage leaders to talk about what they dream about, what they cannot live without, as well as what they cry about. These conversations provide the insights needed to determine the appropriate placement. When a conversation is over, they typically know whether leaders will flourish in the children's department, in the music department, with life groups, or in pastoral care.

A leader's *preparation* begins soon after placement is determined, with each leader experiencing a unique preparation program designed by one of the church's pastors. For example, the program for youth workers goes beyond simply identifying the key competencies and qualities needed in a ministry. It also specifies different development paths for a 16-year old teen than it provides for a 30-year old single mom.

> The pastors are reminded repeatedly that few of the people they work with will look like leaders when they initially encounter them.

Other pastors in charge of various programs have their own lists of key competencies and development plans for that ministry's leaders. The strength of this preparation program is its ability to provide a tailored development path for each individual and each ministry, one that recognizes the unique qualities of every leader.

Promotion of faithful and capable leaders is also part of the development program. While the church appreciates leaders who are task-oriented, they also look for those who display talents that go exceed their job descriptions.

> The quickest way to lose a leader is to have them in the wrong position.

With these leaders, they begin investigating whether they're ready to assume an organizational leadership post. Often this starts by adding oversight of a specific area of their ministry. If the leader is successful there, it might lead to more strategic opportunities involving oversight of an entire ministry and supervising other leaders.

Providing the tools, the training and an investment in leaders is an important component of the development program. Grace purchases whatever curriculum is needed to train its leaders, sends them to conferences, schedules on-site speakers, and exposes them to the ministries of other stellar leaders. The church understands that having leaders who are willing to give their time and talents requires an investment of resources.

Promotion of faithful and capable leaders is also part of the development program.

Beginning with pastoral identification, prayer, placement and preparation, the leaders at Grace are positioned for successful ministry. As they grow, they're continually given opportunities for promotion and provided the tools needed to build effective ministry in God's kingdom.

Teaching Points

- Senior church leaders rely on one of three strategies for accomplishing the work of the ministry:
    - Do-it-yourself – Too much work.
    - Hire it out – Too much money.
    - Develop leaders – Too much time.
- There are a number of reasons today's leaders are not developing others:
    - Pressing demands. Daily responsibilities and the urgency of the moment take our time.
    - Past disappointment. Because we've been hurt, we may not continue developing leaders.
    - Fear of vulnerability. We fear letting others get close enough to us to expose our hearts.
    - Repeating a pattern. Because we were never mentored, we continue the learned pattern of not developing others.
- We have to look for ways to break the cycle.
    - We can begin to seek out mentors and find people.
    - There are many informal mentors who can mentor us through their CDs and books.
    - We have to pass on the blessing of mentoring to the next generation of leaders.
- Don't confuse training with developing.
    - Training focuses on tasks and is less risky.
    - Development focuses on people, not on tasks.
    - We should develop people first, and then train those we've developed.
    - Once someone is developed, they can be trained for a number of tasks.
- Four categories (PEAS) of leadership types can help us

to determine how to best develop them:

- Positional leaders. Have very specific skills. Give them a job.
- Entrepreneurial leaders. Have a pioneer spirit combined with an astute business sense. Give them understanding.
- Administrative leaders. Have the management focus to connect A and B. Give them trust.
- Spiritual leaders. Should be devoting themselves to the Word and to prayer. Give them opportunity.

- Each leadership type has a distinct operating style, different environmental considerations and their own development needs.

- Four development principles will help us to build effective leaders:
  - Know thyself. Distinguishing our own style before developing other leaders guards against making others conform to our style.
  - Build a balanced team. We need a complementary balance among leadership styles.
  - Honor each member. Ensure that each style is able to function and that everyone appreciates the diversity of styles.
  - Unite under a single vision. There can be diversity of function, but not diversity of vision.

- Leadership development cannot occur until we have all of the necessary ingredients.
  - Vision
  - Prayer
  - A plan
  - Opportunity
  - Recognition
  - Time

- Gratitude
- Self-development
- Freedom
- We must also avoid six common leadership killers:
    - Micromanagement
    - Fearful leadership
    - Lack of resources
    - Making failure fatal
    - Creating a glass ceiling
    - Allowing end runs
- Grace Outreach Center develops a leadership culture around the six Ps:
    - Pastoring.
    - Prayer
    - Placement
    - Preparation
    - Promotion
    - Providing

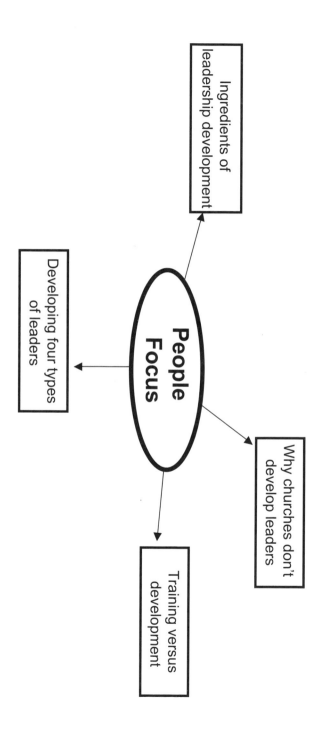

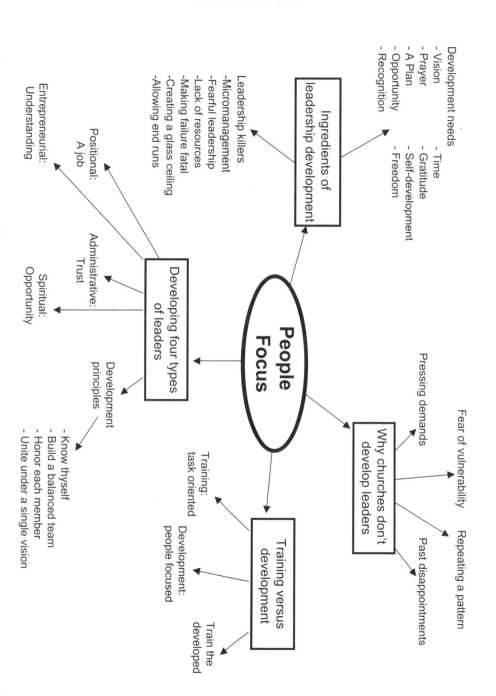

4

Program Focus:
How to Keep Everyone Vision Centered

*Be strong and very courageous. Be careful to obey all the law
my servant Moses gave you; do not turn from it to the right
or to the left, that you may be successful wherever you go.*
-- Joshua 1:7 (New International Version)

Glancing at his watch, Senior Pastor Bill Douglas was glad it was lunchtime. Leaving his tools on the floor of the church narthex, he slowly stretched his arms skyward and straightened his back.

He'd invested hours in refinishing the ancient oak molding that framed this small room, stealing away to his garage workshop to lovingly sand and recoat each one. As he looked admiringly at the gleaming wood, he remembered his small discovery and walked across the room to get it.

Hidden in a corner, he'd found a small plaque. Unable to remove the layers of dust that obscured its engraved contents, he'd placed it aside. Now, with the aid of a rag dipped in cleaning solvent, the words were becoming clearer.

With the grime removed, Bill realized the plaque bore the engraved vision statement of a congregation that had once owned the church building. Reading it, he wondered how many people had been focused on the ensuring the church's success, how many lives had been touched for the Kingdom, and what visible legacy – if any – it left behind.

Drawing the plaque to his chest with both hands, Bill walked into the sanctuary, praying quietly. He'd forgotten all about lunch.

Both people and visions are living, breathing entities with many similarities.

People are not designed to remain unchanged over time; neither are the visions that inspire and motivate them. While their essence remains essentially the same, both can grow, develop and mature. Just as people can experience growth, they can become stagnant, sick and die. Through neglect or a lack of intentional care, visions can also become unhealthy.

> Through neglect or a lack of intentional care, visions can also become unhealthy.

Like people, visions develop in stages. One of the challenges of leadership is keeping everyone focused on the vision that God sets before us. The strength of a ministry is seen in its devotion to a keen, consistent orientation despite the ongoing changes that could thwart progress.

In this chapter, we'll examine the challenges of keeping everyone on the same page, determine how people and organizations can lose their visionary focus, and offer suggestions for recasting a vision in fresh and inspiring ways.

Challenges of Retaining a Visionary Focus

As a vision grows and develops, it progresses through some definite stages:

- During the early genesis or entrepreneurial phase, everyone is excited and gung ho. The enthusiasm in this phase makes it fairly easy to keep everyone on the same page.
- When the vision begins taking shape, some people decide to leave while others drift away. Typically, this happens when people's expectations don't match how the vision is actually coming together.
- As an organization continues to implement a vision, it will attract new people while it weeds out others.
- When the vision matures, the formerly exciting habits or traditions can begin to fossilize. If people cannot be re-engaged so that they're ready to move through another growth cycle – starting again with the genesis phase -- the vision begins to stagnate and die.

> Like people, visions develop in stages.

Every leader grapples with the challenges of keeping people focused through the various stages of a vision. Moving a church forward involves keeping a congregation focused on a vision for the long-term, for 20 years and longer. On-going changes in the composition of the congregation and of the leadership team add to the challenge. It's even more of a struggle to maintain a consistent focus when you have people who've been in the church for 20 years alongside others who have been there for two years. People have a tendency to continue seeing the church like it was when they first came. If the church had 800 people when Joe and Karen joined and now it's tripled in size, Joe and Karen will still think, act and relate as if it still had 800 people. This is true at all levels.

In addition to changes in the leadership team and the congregation, there are many challenges that can cause a church leader to lose sight of where they are and where they're going.

- *Chasing the latest fad.* It's easy for leaders and followers to become impressed by a new book, by the latest teaching, or by the practices of other ministries, especially when they appear more successful than ours. Certainly, we should do all that we can to enhance the growth of God's kingdom in our lives and in our churches. But our primary focus must always be the vision and purpose that God has given to us. We can appreciate what others are doing, but everything we do should be evaluated on the basis of its ability to help or hinder the pursuit of our vision and goals.

  > Every leader grapples with the challenges of keeping people focused through the various stages of a vision.

- *Temptation to embrace an extreme view.* In our zeal to pursue God's ways or eagerness to prove a point, it's easy to adopt an unbalanced position. It doesn't happen overnight and it may not be readily apparent to us. One day, we find ourselves becoming uncharacteristically strict or near the far end of the spectrum on issues. While God might be calling us to be zealous and passionate, we need the humility to stay on the narrow path that is nearest to our goal. We need to be careful about dogmatism on non-essentials.

- *Refusing good ideas.* While we should focus on pursuing our vision, we have to be careful that we're not wearing blinders and refusing what might be beneficial. We need the discernment to know when a new idea might be helpful and when what we're hearing is a distraction.

> People have tendency to continue seeing the church like it was when they first came. If the church had 800 people when Joe and Karen joined and now it's tripled in size, Joe and Karen will still think, act and relate as if it still had 800 people. This is true at all levels.

- *Confusing the urgent with the important.* While He experienced many demands from many people, Jesus consistently discerned what was most important in every situation. Despite the press of a crowd, He could hear the cries of one blind man. We need that same wisdom so that we can hear the still, small voice directing our steps.

- *Listening to the invisible crowd.* When we find ourselves judging every decision or action by the reaction it might produce from others, we're listening to the invisible crowd. While this silent form of peer pressure can be subtle, it's definitely an obstacle to maintaining our focus.

- *Forgetting what God has called us to do.* Churches are filled with needs, with activity, and with work. In this busy and demanding environment, we can lose

> We need to be careful about dogmatism on non-essentials.

the clarity of vision we once had. Ultimately, we

must find ways to ensure that we're committed to accomplishing the vision that God has given us.

How to Regain Focus

A focused leader is the key to a focused organization. If the senior leader loses his or her way, the results trickle through the entire organization. These organizational dynamics are expressed in various ways:

- When the senior pastor gets bored, the organization gets stagnant.
- When the senior pastor begins to drift, the organization becomes confused.
- When the senior pastor grows indifferent, the organization is ineffective.

Whatever focus there is in our churches is directly related to our own focus. Unless God is leading us somewhere else, we have to remain consistent. While the urge might be powerful

> A focused leader is the key to a focused organization.

at times, we cannot afford to put the ministry on cruise control.

Maintaining our balance in life is essential. Throughout His life, Jesus always had balance. He knew when to rebuke and when to refrain, when to heal and when to withhold, when to push on and when to stay put. He never struggled to find the critical balance in any moment. When we're becoming unfocused, it's because we're struggling to find a balance between the following areas:

- Spiritual and natural
- Style and substance
- Popular and proven
- Major and minor

No one loses his or her focus overnight; it happens gradually over a period of time. It's also likely that it's the result of a combination of daily, ministry-related challenges and personal pressures. Like any malady, there are observable signs and symptoms that we're beginning to lose our way:

- Compassion fatigue
- Crisis-mode living
- Complacency
- Cynicism

- **Compassion fatigue.** Pastors are thrown into many tough environments. Dealing with people's lives requires great emotional energy. When you're young and starting out, you have higher levels of energy overall. A steady diet of challenges becomes draining. That's when compassion fatigue sets in.

When we've heard so many stories from people who are struggling with divorce, people fighting life-threatening illness, and battling with emotional problems, it begins to affect us. If we don't learn the meaning and importance of detachment, we can become casualties. If we don't learn to pull back, we won't survive. Detachment doesn't mean that we don't care, or that we don't re-engage. It's a tool that helps us to retain our objectivity and

> No one loses his or her focus overnight; it happens gradually over a period of time.

conserve our emotional strength so that we're able to engage with everyone who needs us. To remain healthy, every leader has to practice detached concern, concern without unhealthy attachment.

We can protect ourselves from compassion fatigue by making sure that we take periodic vacations. Scripture shows us that Jesus took many breaks during his three-and-a-half year ministry. Not many pastors follow that healthy practice because we become so engulfed by the ministry. We all need to schedule breaks, to disappear for a vacation at the beach or some time in the mountains. It's important to plan those breaks *before* we think we need them. If we wait until we think we need them, we may never get around to it. Without that rest, we can succumb to compassion fatigue and compromise our effectiveness.

> A steady diet of challenges becomes draining.

- **Crisis-Mode Living.** We're easily drawn into every crisis that the church is going through. We get involved in problems caused by insufficient offerings, issues with the building program, and the troubles of people threatening to leave. Just when we think we've got one thing under control, we have to get the prayer meeting organized, ensure that we're taking care of whatever issues our staff has identified and still find time to prepare the sermon. Rather than working from a predetermined list of priorities, it seems like we're just living from one crisis to another. This type of crisis-mode living is a close cousin of compassion fatigue.

> If we don't learn the meaning and importance of detachment, we can become casualties.

When we're stuck in crisis-mode living, we need a restoration of faith. We cannot afford to regard everything as a problem. When we're empowered by the spirit of faith, out attitude becomes "we believe and therefore speak[11]." But without the right attitude, everything is magnified; little problems become big problems, and all we see is more money, more people, and more work. Without this faith-filled attitude, a new ministry opportunity that can help us reach hundreds of kids becomes just another chore and just another fundraising effort.

> ...without the right attitude, everything is magnified; little problems become big problems...

- **Complacency.** When the church is no longer fighting for survival, when the programs and leaders we've established are working well, there are still subtle dangers that can blur or distort our focus. It happens as we become comfortable in our activities and they become routine. Like a car operating on cruise control, we begin operating without much effort or energy. We are present in body, but we are absent in spirit.

This type of mental and emotional fatigue requires a defibrillator shock to rouse us from our complacency. We can typically find this remedy in the company of visionary people.

Dr. Chand's Perspective

For me, it's not what I read or my prayer life that

causes complacency to retreat. What compels me forward is being around energized visionaries. By watching and listening to them, I find myself reinvigorated and encouraged.

If we're mentoring a young leader, or helping someone who's in a different season of ministry, being around these folks can also help us to regain the thrill. We might find that their company and their zeal begins fanning the flames of our own vision.

Sometimes, our focus is so intense that it's helpful to go somewhere else for encouragement. At conferences -- like the North Texas Leadership Conference held every October in Plano, Texas – we can find our own vision refreshed as we fellowship with others immersed in visionary journeys. At places like this, we can form friendships with peers who can provide us with a "relationship burst" when we're home and falling into complacency.

- **Cynicism.** Even Moses grew cynical and disillusioned. Because of what he witnessed about human nature in Israel, he battled with his own doubts. He complained to God about the people or angrily struck the rock twice to produce water for these stubborn followers.

Likewise, our own over-exposure to human nature can produce cynicism. After we've been burned by irresponsible or undependable actions, we might begin to doubt that anyone keeps their word. After yet-another Sunday school teacher fails to show up or another prayer meeting remains unattended, we grow skeptical of others' promises and motives. We say we're just being realistic, but the roots of cynicism need precious little nurturing. Gradually, we stop believing the best about people. And when

> ...the roots of cynicism need precious little nurturing...

we view everyone we're leading as just another problem, where can we possibly be taking them?

Again, the story of Moses presents a solution. At one point, God tells Moses that He's ready to wipe out Israel and start over again with Moses. Apparently, this produces fresh love for the people in Moses, and he pleads with God to spare them. Just as Moses experienced a rebirth that freed him from cynicism, we may need to pray for the same Divine surgery to free us.

Enhancing the Focus of the Ministry Team

In addition to continually maintaining our own visionary focus, a senior pastor must prevent a loss of vision on the ministry team. We can ensure that other leaders retain clarity of vision by providing them with:

- Fresh moments
- Fresh eyes
- Fresh fun

*By offering **fresh moments**,* we're giving the team an opportunity to get away from ministry needs and view things from another perspective. We can accomplish this in a number of ways:

- Whether it involves one service or a few days, taking an outside speaking opportunity can help a team member to get recharged. Encourage them if they have opportunities to speak at a conference or a workshop, or even to speak at another church.
- We can also send them to a ministry conference, a retreat, or to specialized training.
- Not all churches can afford to send the staff away for training. In those cases, it's helpful to bring in a speaker or consultant who can work with the whole team. This also has the advantage of renewing the entire staff, instead of just one or two people.

If these fresh moments provide our team with a renewed vision, they're worth the price we have to pay.

Fresh eyes *are needed* to keep people engaged. Having the team engaged with a leadership

Teams are built in two ways -- crisis and fun – choose fun.

consultant can also provide important input for them. An external evaluation of the ministry helps them see things more objectively, replacing perplexity with purity.

Another set of fresh eyes are your new employees and new members. These fresh eyes will become old eyes after three months, when they blend into the existing fabric and adopt your present DNA and conform to the culture.

We cannot neglect **fresh fun.** Periodically scheduling time together that's not focused on the work of the ministry is an important aspect of team building. A casual meal, a few hours away together, or a regular social activity can go a long way toward building cohesiveness, teamwork, and enhancing the clarity of everyone's vision. Teams are built in two ways – crisis and fun – choose fun.

Finding Fresh Ways to Recast the Vision

Even secular companies recognize the importance of re-packaging goods and services and marketing them in new ways. Why else would we have so many varieties of Coke and Pepsi?

Finding fresh ways to present our vision invites participation. We don't have to have the budget of a Fortune 500 company to communicate in new and exciting ways. At The Church on the Way, Jack Hayford simply changes the look of his stage by rebuilding it, repainting and surrounding the platform with new plants. Why does he go through this process three times a year? Because he's discovered that creating this sense of newness fosters expectancy, providing an entry in people's souls and minds. Many churches, like Salem Fields Community Church in Fredericksburg, VA, create new stage sets for each sermon series.

> ...we have to understand that it's easy to mistake a new idea for a vision.

Creating new enthusiasm over our vision doesn't necessarily require a trip to Home Depot. There are raw materials all around us – in the hearts and minds of our leadership team and our congregation. Our willingness to renovate and explore the new ideas and suggestions that come our way can provide fresh avenues on the road to accomplishing our purpose

Before we undertake this building process, we have to understand that it's easy to mistake a new idea for a vision.

Something new always seems better and more exciting than what's already in progress.

Think about what happens after someone on the ministry team returns from a conference. After hearing some hot new idea, he or she talks excitedly about the blessings of implementing this direction. While your leader might be right, new directions that are not properly channeled could cause the church to be pushed and pulled by every new wind that comes along. Before long, you'll be blown off course.

Handled properly, however, we can leverage an encounter with someone brimming with new ideas so that we emerge encouraged, with fresh opportunities to recast our vision. And we can accomplish this without squelching new concepts or extinguishing godly enthusiasm.

The most important step is clearly understanding the boundaries of our vision. Getting boundaries right is vital. The first leadership failure was Adam's and Eve's refusal to acknowledge the boundaries God had given when He said, "Don't touch this tree." When Joshua was released in the ministry, he established boundaries by saying, "You will possess this land from this place to this." Every leader should communicate the boundaries of what they're called to do, conveying this information clearly and regularly.

> Getting boundaries right is vital. Having a firm understanding of our boundaries makes it easier to evaluate new ideas and recast them in a helpful fashion.

Having a firm understanding of our boundaries makes it easier to evaluate new ideas and recast them in a helpful fashion. Let's say you're attending an event together with your leadership team. At dinner you can begin to facilitate a discussion about how the ideas you're hearing might fit within your boundaries. Over dinner, you could say, "We've heard a hundred good ideas. But what we need to explore is which ideas complement our vision. Here are the parameters of our vision. What fits and what doesn't?"

If the conversation gets off track, you can redirect it by clarifying the intent for attending this event. "We didn't come to this conference to begin implementing new programs for cell groups. We came there to see what's being done that can work within our framework."

Once a senior leader has facilitated this discussion, everyone will understand which new ideas fit with the vision, which simplifies the task of communicating with the church. You can decide what to present and determine what needs further investigation and prayer. This type

> ...the most important meeting is the meeting that happens before the meeting.

of conversation and planning make it much easier to keeps everyone's vision fresh and focused.

If Moses used this approach with the 12 spies reporting their reconnaissance mission into the Promised Land, it would have prevented problems. Unfortunately, Moses forgot something important: the most important meeting is the meeting that happens *before* the meeting. Just imagine what might have occurred if he had facilitated a session with this team *before* they spoke to the people. He might have discovered fresh ways to help these leaders integrate the information they had into their God-given direction. It might have helped them to stay centered on their vision.

Teaching Points

- One of the challenges of leadership is keeping everyone focused on the vision that God sets before us.
- On-going changes in the composition of the congregation and of the leadership team add to the challenge.
- Many challenges cause a leader to lose sight of where they are headed:
  - Chasing the latest fad.
  - Temptation to embrace an extreme view.
  - Refusing good ideas.
  - Confusing the urgent with the important.
  - Listening to the invisible crowd.
  - Forgetting what God has called us to do.
- If the senior leader loses his or her way, the results trickle through the entire organization.
- There are observable signs and symptoms of losing one's way:
  - Compassion fatigue. A steady diet of challenges becomes draining.
  - Crisis-mode living. We're easily drawn into every crisis that the church is going through.
  - Complacency. Even when we've reached a level of success, we can still become fatigued.
  - Cynicism. After we've been burned by irresponsible or undependable actions, we might begin to doubt that anyone keeps their word.
- We can ensure that other leaders retain their clarity of vision by providing them with:

- Fresh moments to gain another perspective.
- Fresh eyes to them engaged.
- Fresh fun to build a team spirit.
- Creating a sense of newness can foster expectancy.
  - Having a firm understanding of our boundaries makes it easier to evaluate new ideas and recast them in a helpful fashion.

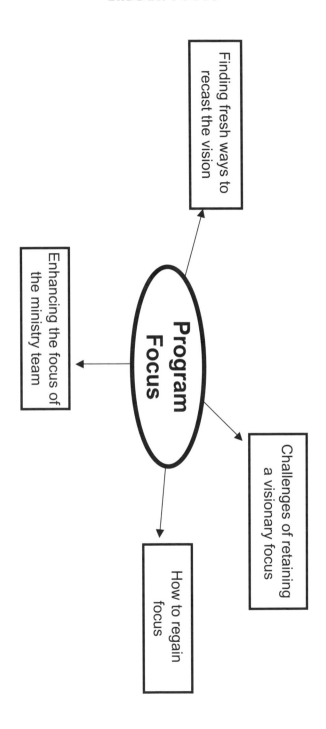

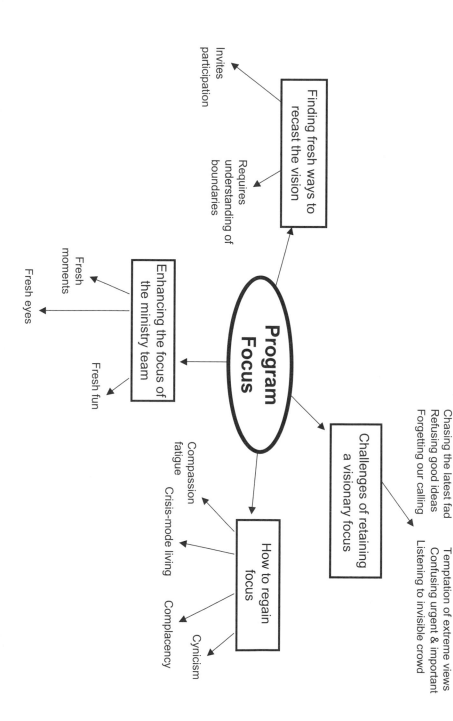

5

Procedural Focus:
How to Grow a Fit and Trim Organization

Seest thou a man diligent in his business?
He shall stand before kings.
-- Proverbs 22:29 (King James Version)

Pastor Jake Barrett stepped out his front door and closed it quietly behind him. Putting his house key into the front pocket of his sweat suit, he knelt to tighten the laces on his running shoes.

While stretching, he began debating that morning's exercise strategy. Always a competitive runner, Jake had recently injured his knee preparing for an upcoming race. In an attempt to shave a few minutes off his time, he'd adopted a strenuous training regimen that was apparently not well suited to the mountainous area where he lived and ran. According to his physician, his training strategy was also inappropriate for a man in his fifties.

While Jake knew the doctor was right, he also knew that he loved running a fast mile, breaking past other runners and beating his own best time. A few weeks of letting the injury heal had given Jake ample time to reassess his exercise goals. At his age, was it necessary to be the fastest? Could he be satisfied with not being overweight, with having excellent blood pressure readings, and an enjoyable way to relieve his stress? In the end, he wondered if his overemphasis on results was unhealthy.

Catching himself automatically reaching to set the timer on his sports watch, Jake stopped and smiled. Jogging slowly down the street, he smiled and waved at a passing neighbor. He knew there would be no timed miles that morning.

Have you ever walked into a church or an organization and sensed the tension in the air? It didn't matter what else you experienced there, you just couldn't shake that feeling and those vibes. You intuitively felt the high stress levels and knew that the people were overworked.

While there are a variety of reasons for this, the cause can frequently be attributed to an overemphasis on results. If we want functional – rather than dysfunctional -- organizations, it's vital that we make their health more important than their functionality. We're not suggesting that we should ignore functionality -- only that it should be properly prioritized.

> It's vital that we make health more important than functionality

This type of organizational stress can begin when a well-meaning leader imports systems from other churches that have impressed him or her. Regardless of how effective that other church's by-laws, policies and procedures might be, they cannot simply be imported and transplanted. They must match our own church's demographics and style. Just as we cannot import revival, we cannot import organizational effectiveness.

Whatever systems we adopt should always be contextualized to our community. It's not enough to know that it played well in Peoria; there has to be a DNA match to our own organization. By focusing on *why* a church or organization does something instead of focusing only on *what* they're doing, we can facilitate this matching and customization. This simple change in our thinking helps us to grasp the essence of a procedure or a program, which enables us to have the new ideas that we'll need to build effective systems.

> Whatever systems we adopt should always be contextualized to our community.

In this chapter, we'll focus on additional ways to build and maintain healthy organizations by examining the procedural areas that can increase or undermine organizational effectiveness. You'll discover ways to evaluate organizational vital signs, recognize the symptoms of developing problems, address issues around hiring procedures, and learn ways to build effective teams.

Implementing an Evaluation System

An effective evaluation system enables a leader to regularly audit how current policies and procedures are affecting the on-going health of an organization and its employees. As evaluations are completed, the necessary adjustments can be made.

The evaluation systems themselves can range from informal conversations to the more sophisticated performance-management systems used by many corporations. In some organizations, an informal system might work well, while others need a more structured approach, and still others can utilize any combination of the following evaluation methods:

- Informal Systems
- Personal Development Plans
- Strategic Reports

Informal Systems. Some churches and organizations find that they're able to function well without a policy manual or an associated evaluation model. In Dr. Brooks' church, for example, every leader is encouraged to think and function at the leadership level, which means going beyond job descriptions. If they encounter lights left on in buildings after services or meetings are over, they don't immediately assign it as someone's job to ensure the lights are turned off. They expect any leader who's present to take ownership of the situation and turn them out.

> A written PDP offers an effective method for charting progress.

In order for this informal method to work well, however, we have to assume that everyone is functioning at the leadership level. We have to assume that every leader is continually asking the question, "What can I do?" rather than "What's my job?".

When leaders operate at this level, measuring the bottom line is relatively simple, which makes evaluations informal and intuitive. They can be based on behaviors that you observe, feedback you might receive and apparent growth that you witness.

Personal Development Plans. Dr. Chand frequently recommends that leaders create a personal development plan (PDP) to track their goals. While many leaders have a development plan, they typically don't put it in writing. It's essential to have a written PDP, since having it in that format offers a more effective method for charting progress.

A PDP can be used to measure progress in many categories, such as areas in a leader's personal life, spiritual development and educational plans. It can include what they're going to read, how often they'll see a mentor, conferences they'll attend, periodicals they'll subscribe to, and CDs they'll listen to.

In any category, a leader can identify a topic or an issue that they want or need to explore or develop further. They might want to further develop a particular strength or to grow in an area where they need additional development. The plan should detail the specifics in each area.

Once the plan is created, it can be discussed with the leader's supervisor. When examining a leader's PDP, check for areas where they can be more specific, clarify their goals and link them to the organizational vision. For example, one executive pastor that Dr. Chand works with added a weight loss goal in the personal development category of his PDP. While he had some good strategies, he neglected to mention how frequently he planned to exercise at the gym.

> We have to assume that every leader is continually asking the question, "What can I do?" rather than "What's my job?".

After a PDP is finalized for each leader, it should be used to track their progress during a regular evaluation cycle.

Strategic Reports. Twice each year, the leaders at Dr. Brooks' church are required to write a strategic analysis of the ministries they lead, which are shared with the church board. Each analysis evaluates the ministry's past, present and future in the following areas:

- *Numbers.* If ministries have attendance, conversion or other figures associated with them, the leaders must provide historical details and offer future projections. They might say, "The ministry was averaging X a year ago, is averaging Y right now and I expect it to be averaging Z in the future."
- *Success and failure.* Leaders are also expected to provide descriptions of any fruitful creative efforts and to report on ideas they've tried that have not worked. For less-than-successful efforts, they typically provide information about how they've handled those results. The reports also offer information on ministries that are pioneering in areas that are not expected to immediately become fruitful or productive.
- *Leadership development.* The reports also list the new leaders that are being developed by the current leadership, as well as any potential leaders they may be considering.
- *Reading.* Each leader is required to list the books and the journals they've read and describe how they've contributed to their development.

Before the report is presented to the board, both the executive and senior pastors evaluate each leader's report. The reports facilitate on-going communication and provide a number of advantages:

- Each report offers an opportunity to give personal feedback to each leader, to clarify facts, and to suggest areas where development may be needed.
- The church maintains a valuable leadership resource by regularly identifying potential leaders and tracking those who are currently in the leadership development program.
- On-going course corrections are easier when there's a history of successful and less-than-fruitful efforts.
- Ministries that have numbers associated with them gain the ability to chart their seasons of growth and identify additional development opportunities.
- With the facts in hand, it's also easier to abandon pioneering efforts when no long-term success is becoming evident.

Watching for Signs of an Unhealthy Organization

You might know someone whose diet consists primarily of fast food, who doesn't exercise regularly, and seems to be wearing larger-sized clothes every time you see him. Unless he changes his ways, you don't need a medical degree to predict his on-coming collision with some major health problems. Your friend is never going to be healthy as long as he keeps practicing these unhealthy habits.

Unhealthy practices don't develop overnight.

Unhealthy practices don't develop overnight. Gradually, someone who travels a lot on business finds that she's eating more junk food because it's easier to find. Over time, demands at work and at home make it harder for her to get to the gym. Before long, the fast-food diet and a lack of exercise results in a larger waist size, high blood pressure, and open the door to other health problems. If you don't know what to look for, the early symptoms can easily sneak by.

Maintaining a healthy organization also involves an awareness of symptoms of on-coming problems. Even the healthiest of churches can develop small habits that undermine its wellness over time. Knowing what to look for and avoid can help us to make a difference.

In our experience, unhealthy organizations demonstrate one or more of the following symptoms:

- An ignorance of exit traffic
- Limited involvement from the senior pastor
- Low levels of staff loyalty
- Promotions based on tenure rather than talent

- *An ignorance of exit traffic.* It's unfortunate when churches have no idea why people are leaving. Even when functioning members stop attending, there are no clear policies or procedures for following up with them. They can't tell whether they lost two percent or twenty percent over the previous six-month period, let alone identify why. Even churches that are experiencing growth are not exempt. If they don't get a handle on their exit traffic, they're headed for a health problem that's going

> Unhealthy practices don't develop overnight.

to limit and affect that growth. It might take a while to detect, but it will become evident.

- *Limited involvement from the senior pastor.* Some pastors are off speaking so much that they're uninformed about what's going on in their own churches. If you want to find them, don't bother looking in their offices because they're never there. Taking speaking invitations is good, but we have to ensure that it's balanced and that it's not done in an attitude of avoidance.

> Even the healthiest of churches can develop small habits that undermine its wellness over time.

There's a fine line between delegation and dumping responsibility. While the senior pastor should delegate some responsibility, there are certain duties that should not be given away. Too much delegation is a sign that the senior pastor is disengaged.

It's never healthy when others in leadership are aware of problems that the senior pastor is not. If a situation blows up and the senior pastor is surprised, it demonstrates how uninvolved he's become.

In addition to being fully engaged, the senior pastor should be an active, inquisitive learner. How can we expect to be effective teachers and responsible leaders if we're not actively learning? Too many times, we're only reading books and articles that rehash the same materials and the same doctrine. Reviewing the same material is not learning. Learning assumes confronting something new, it involves variety, and it means journeying into new areas.

The senior pastor also needs to be fully engaged in preaching. As Jack Hayford recommends, we should follow a preaching plan that covers the fundamentals of the faith over a two-year period. And our preaching should be mainly expository preaching rather than topical. An overemphasis on topical preaching can become unhealthy. Expository preaching produces Bible-taught believers.

> It's never healthy when others in leadership are aware of problems that the senior pastor is not.

- *Low levels of staff loyalty.* You can learn a lot about the health of a church by discerning the attitudes of the senior pastor's staff. If there are strong undercurrents rather than a sense of loyalty and support, it can suggest larger problems.

  Leaders who want to create a sense of unity in their efforts can end up stifling the staff and creating a dictatorial tone. Even when someone's efforts are successful, they make sure that nothing is ever done again without their permission. A continuation of this negative response eventually stifles communication altogether and creates a culture of fear, intimidation and control. No one wants to tell these leaders anything, which can result in very unhealthy situations.

- *Promotions based on tenure rather than talent.* Sometimes, what happens in churches is no different than what happens in government agencies and Fortune 500 companies. There are bureaucrats in some jobs who don't fit in any longer.

> Expository preaching produces Bible-taught believers.

However, because they've been there for so long and their management doesn't want to challenge or confront them, they play it safe and promote them into another position.

While these actions are understandable, they're also creating an unhealthy environment. They send a signal that it's not always talent or abilities that are rewarded. And once we begin rewarding mediocrity, where does it stop?

> ...once we begin rewarding mediocrity, where does it stop?

All organizations – including churches -- need to face the fact that their old leaders will seldom become their new leaders. Someone who is tied to yesterday's solutions will only become today's problem. There should be a constant renewal of young and old based on the ability to keep the organization moving forward. Transferring people somewhere else is not a solution.

Imagine someone waking up from cancer surgery in the operating room. When she sees the surgeon, she immediately asks, "Did you get it all?". What if the answer she got was, "Well, it was too difficult to remove. We carved the cancer cells into little pieces and placed them in different body parts." Unfortunately, that's exactly what we do when we transfer people to other departments every time they don't work out.

> Someone who is tied to yesterday's solutions will only become today's problem.

Military leaders understand this. If there's a second lieutenant causing problems in a brigade or a battalion, the general never agrees to transfer him to another battalion. If they transfer their problems to another battalion, the other battalions get word of it and begin transferring their problems to the offender. It's an unwritten law that you deal with problems; you don't transfer them because it only makes things worse.

Organizations with a heavy family influence have to be especially careful that they're focused on validating and rewarding talent over time. If they don't, it just begins looking like "the family business," which only creates an unhealthy "us against them" mentality. If our ministry includes other family members, we should make an extra effort to establish and underscore strong lines of accountability and continually demonstrate that we reward and validate talent.

> It's an unwritten law that you deal with problems; you don't transfer them because it only makes things worse.

It requires effort and watchfulness to maintain a healthy organization, just as it does to ensure our own personal health. Having an understanding of symptoms and taking the necessary corrective actions can help to build effective, functional organizations.

Addressing Hiring Issues

Good leaders tend to be trusting individuals. When someone is part of our team, we trust them, which is an essential part of effective leadership. But trust has a downside; it comes with blind spots. Many good leaders have been blindsided because they trusted too much. When that happens, we naturally wonder if we should stop being so trusting. But shutting down a trusting nature isn't easy and it isn't natural. The right thing to do is to continue trusting within certain boundaries. We have to work at establishing our boundaries and making them consistent with our values.

One way to establish those boundaries is to make someone else responsible for hiring and firing and to establish clear lines of authority within the organization. Putting someone else in charge of this responsibility keeps us from fighting with our trusting nature, that part of us that can make it difficult to execute the difficult decisions that often surround hiring and firing.

> Many good leaders have been blindsided because they trusted too much.

At Great Outreach Center, the church's executive pastor handles these staffing decisions. Dr. Brooks clearly sees the benefits of giving someone else this responsibility. As the church grew, it freed him from making time-consuming staffing decisions and enabled him to invest time in other areas. When he's traveling, he can relax in the knowledge that someone else has the authority to keep things running smoothly.

One hiring issue that many churches are wrestling with centers on whether it's better for them to promote from within or to hire someone from the outside. Dr. Chand typically recommends following the example of many healthy organizations, which first look inside for a qualified candidate before searching externally. If no candidates are found inside, then looking outside is a legitimate option.

Those who want to hire and promote only from within think that insiders are better suited because they already understand the church culture and its operations. This paternalistic hiring philosophy appears to have more disadvantages than benefits. Only hiring from within might match your organizational DNA; just keep in mind that it can also result in:

> The goal of every hiring process should be to find the best-qualified person...

- *Slower growth.* When Grace was limited to hiring internal candidates, the church grew at a slower pace. When they realized that they needed people with experience and skills beyond what they presently had, they began looking externally. In the end, they found that hiring believers who had worked in corporate settings satisfied many of their needs.
- *In-fighting.* Rather than simplifying a search, limiting hiring to internal candidates can actually complicate matters. Once the policy is known, people will begin jockeying for position, which is not the type of motivation we want to encourage. When only one internal candidate is selected, it can also create awkward situations, uncomfortable feelings and resentment among those who weren't chosen.
- *A limited pool of candidates.* Hiring from within limits the number of qualified people. For example, let's say that we're looking for a person to handle accounting and need someone who is a CPA. In addition to looking within our own ranks for a CPA, this person also has to meet the qualifications of church membership, and have a willingness to leave their outside job and come to work for a church. We might be searching for a needle in a haystack.

Focusing on the internal/external debate, however, avoids addressing the most important issue: finding and hiring the best possible candidate. The goal of every hiring process should be to find the best-qualified person – regardless of where they come from. To do that, we must be very clear about the job's requirements and qualifications. The clearer the profile, the better are our chances of finding the right person. If we have people on the search team who are still tied to the idea of internal hiring, a clear job description can stop this debate by making it clear that we don't have a candidate inside the church.

> The clearer the profile, the better are our chances of finding the right person.

By not imposing limits on hiring searches, we open ourselves up to God's provision. Whether the right person comes from within the church or transfers in from the business world, we'll have the right combination of talent and strength to move the church forward.

Developing a Winning Team

In the 2004 Olympics, the United States basketball team boasted a number of NBA stars. They had players from the Lakers, from the Knicks, and from the Nuggets. But despite the team's impressive line-up, they lost to teams from Puerto Rico, from Lithuania, and from Argentina. Having great players doesn't necessarily mean that you have a winning team.

Mediocre players who are a great team will beat great players who form a mediocre team.

Turning an array of star players into a great team requires

adopting a coach's attitude. Being a coach doesn't mean we start wearing a whistle and expecting everyone to run laps around the sanctuary. There are three ways that a coach's attitude can help us to build a winning a team:

1. Having appropriate expectations.
2. Keeping the focus on common goals, not on style.
3. Treating everyone fairly.

1. *Having appropriate expectations.* We can and should expect every leader on our team to have some similar basic knowledge. For example, everyone should be able to communicate the church's vision, to know how their particular position enhances that vision, and to conduct their daily responsibilities in a way that moves the church toward achieving our vision.

> Having great players doesn't necessarily mean that you have a winning team.

But expecting everyone to understand and adhere to the playbook doesn't mean that everyone is going to play at the same level. We have people with different levels of experience, different backgrounds, and different gifts. We can't expect that each of them will deliver on that in the same way. We have to recognize and appreciate their individual differences.

2. *Keeping the focus on goals, not on style.* Adopting a coach's attitude means keeping everyone focused on the same goal. That means that the senior pastor should regularly meet with the entire team to ensure that the vision is being communicated in our current efforts. That vision should be part of small groups, of our services, of special care we provide, and of every-

thing else we do. It's the senior pastor's job to ensure that the vision is an integral part of every effort.

Once that goal is understood, we shouldn't put limitations on how a leader accomplishes it. Too many of us confuse vision and style. One of the biggest errors comes from expecting everyone to do things the same way, or to be exactly like us. While we can require everyone to operate within the boundaries set by the vision, we should not put limitations on style. In the end, their style is probably suited to the ministry they're overseeing. Depending on the person and the ministry, their style might be more emotional, more analytical, or more creative. As long as each individual leader is enhancing the vision and shooting at the same target, how they do that is best left up to them.

> It's the senior pastor's job to ensure that the vision is an integral part of every effort.

3. *Treating everyone fairly.* Coaching is a skill that involves distinguishing the people on the team that need our time and attention. We don't have to spend the same amount of time with each person. A youth pastor that has been with us for 14 years doesn't require the same amount of attention and interaction that a new staff person might require. That youth pastor probably requires very little oversight. But before that new person begins reflecting our vision and values, it's going to require additional time and attention. We might want to include them in various meetings and take them to breakfast or lunch. We

> We don't have to treat everyone equally in order to treat them fairly.

won't ignore the youth pastor; we'll only provide him or her with a bit less time. We don't have to treat everyone equally in order to treat them fairly.

Developing and implementing coaching skills is an integral part of team building. It requires us to focus on serving our leaders, being acquainted with their abilities, and assisting them as they use their God-given ministry gifts to help the church achieve its vision.

Teaching Points

- It's vital that we make the health of our organizations more important than their functionality.
- An effective evaluation system enables a regular audit of on-going health.
- We can utilize any combination of the following evaluation methods:
    - Informal Systems. Some churches are able to function well without a policy manual or an associated evaluation model.
    - Personal Development Plans. A written PDP offers an effective method for charting progress.
    - Strategic Reports. Regular reports facilitate ongoing communication about past, present and future.
- Maintaining a healthy organization also involves an awareness of symptoms of on-coming problems.
- Unhealthy organizations demonstrate one or more of the following symptoms:
    - An ignorance of exit traffic.
    - Limited involvement from the senior pastor.
    - Low levels of staff loyalty.
    - Promotions based on tenure rather than talent.
- Many churches are wrestling with whether to promote from within or to hire from the outside.
- Limiting hiring to insiders has certain disadvantages:
    - Slower growth
    - In-fighting
    - A limited pool of candidates
- The goal of any hiring process should be to find the best candidate, regardless of where they come from.

- Turning star players into a great team involves having a coach's attitude:
    - Having appropriate expectations.
    - Keeping the focus on common goals, not on style.
    - Treating everyone fairly.

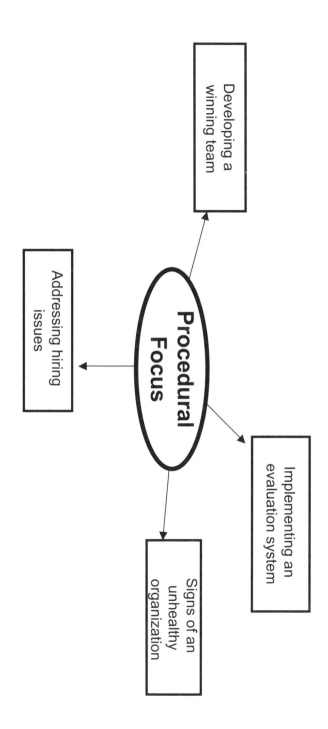

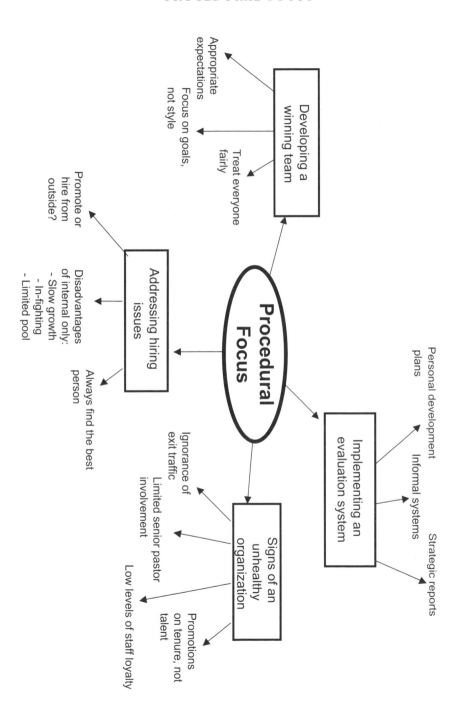

6

Problem Focus:
How to Stay on Target in a Crisis

Shall we accept good from God, and not trouble?
-- Job 2:10 (New International Version)

If you falter in times of trouble, how small is your strength!
-- Proverbs 24:10 (New International Version)

Walking through the parking lot behind city hall, Pastor Bill Douglas pressed the unlock button on his key ring and opened the door to his SUV. Once inside, he sat quietly without turning on the ignition.

It had been nearly a year since the first, hasty meeting of guidance counselors, psychologists, and law enforcement officers convened to deal with issues surrounding an aborted school shooting. Invited because of the size of the church's youth group, Bill was the only pastor in the group. Because he was likely the only believer, he frequently found himself at odds with some of the proposed solutions and thinking. Bill managed to get through some of the more heated discussions, taking a firm stand yet without alienating anyone.

At the last few sessions, Bill discovered how much he had grown to respect the others in spite of their differing views. Together, they had seen a potential crisis through and grown closer as a result. Despite his feelings that he had little influence in the group, two of the others had voluntarily asked him about the times of church services.

Turning on the ignition, Bill wondered whether their interest was sincere or they were just being polite. "Time will tell," he thought, as he backed the SUV out of the parking space.

A crisis. An on-going trial. A rapidly escalating problem. What happens when you read those words? For many of us, they can produce unpleasant memories of past events, troubling thoughts or emotions.

It's critical that all leaders understand that a crisis doesn't have to produce an entirely negative experience. We can look at Joseph, at Daniel, and at countless other Scriptural examples to see that God often uses a crisis to elevate a leader.

A crisis in the church can transform a preacher into a pastor. When a minister arrives at a new pastorate, he's their preacher. It takes a few years for him to earn the trust of the congregation and become their pastor. A crisis can accelerate that timeline, as it did for Dr. Chand.

Dr. Chand's Experience

In 1980, I began pastoring a church in Michigan. Quite unexpectedly, I learned that the worship leader's wife – Charlene – was experiencing some severe health problems. One night, one of their kids called the parsonage to say, "Please be praying for my mom. She is at the Mayo Clinic in Rochester, Minnesota, and she's going to have emergency surgery on a brain tumor tomorrow morning."

Bill, who was the worship leader, had already driven his wife there and was now waiting by himself. This was before cell phones, so there was no easy way for me to reach him. I didn't have much money, as my salary was a little more than one hundred dollars a week. But I knew I had to do something. Since the banks were closed, I went to one of the elders and asked him for a loan so that I could drive my little Mazda up to Rochester. I told him that my wife would go to the bank and repay him the next day.

Bill had a lot of family in the church. His twin sister was the church secretary, his parents were members, and his dad even served on the board. Despite this, no one asked me to go to the hospital in Rochester, Minnesota. The only information I had was from a phone call from his 15-year old son who asked me to pray.

Together with my trusty map, I left late in the evening and drove all night to get to the Mayo Clinic. When I walked into the hospital, I found Bill alone, pacing back and forth. When he saw me, he ran across the room, and grabbed me in a hug. Despite his being about 15 years older than me, he began crying and crying, and saying, "Thank you so much for coming."

Back then, you could rent a bedroom and a shared bath across the street from the clinic for about $12 a night. Since neither of us had much money, Bill and I shared a room, sleeping in the same bed for three or four nights. When Charlene was out of danger, I drove back to Michigan.

When I got home, there was such an outpouring of love from the people in the church. Bill's relatives came by the parsonage to give me money, despite my insistence that it hadn't cost me that much and that money wasn't an issue. In just a few months, that crisis turned me into a pastor and knitted me together with many of my best supporters.

When we act consistently with our belief in the sovereignty of God and the knowledge that the steps of a righteous man are ordered by the Lord[12], we become open to new opportunities. As God empowers us to overcome, even being in the lion's den can be transformed into a positive experience.

If we examine history – whether we're talking about global, national, local, or church history – we see that leaders are discovered in times of crisis. You don't necessarily find leaders during good times; they arise during the tough times, during the challenging times. Think about Martin Luther King Jr., Winston Churchill, Mahatma Gandhi and Rudy Giuliani; each of these leaders was elevated into a very visible and memorable role during a particular crisis. What we do and how we compose ourselves during a crisis will be remembered long after our best sermons. People will remember us being there, walking with them as they walk through the valley of the shadow of death. They won't forget that. These times can forge bonds like nothing else can.

> ...leaders are discovered in times of crisis.

In this chapter, we'll examine ways to analyze and respond to a crisis, discuss methods for building support, and learn how to be better prepared for a crisis.

Analyzing Levels of Crisis

An inherent level of confusion and noise characterizes many crises. Because we may have to quickly decide among many choices, a chorus of voices will be offering unsolicited advice. But a leader cannot – and should not -- listen to everyone.

All leaders should understand that not all problems are equal, nor do they deserve the same degree of attention. By understanding the various levels of a crisis, we can determine how involved the senior pastor should be. We should distinguish between the following levels of crisis:

- Personal crisis
- People crisis
- Public crisis
- Problem crisis
- Pressure crisis

- **A personal crisis** is fairly easy to recognize. For many senior leaders, the greatest crises are not those occurring in the church but those that are affecting them or their family, leaving them feeling vulnerable. For Dr. Brooks, the toughest time in his ministry was when one of his children was having open-heart surgery.

> ...not all problems are equal, nor do they deserve the same degree of attention.

A personal crisis might also have a professional component. We may find that we're no longer being satisfied in our current duties, or are facing the limits of our competence in certain areas. We can be facing the professional pain of our limitations described by the Peter Principle. We know that we've risen to our highest level of incompetence.

> ...we have to lead on a personal level as well as on the public level.

Times of personal crisis can be particularly difficult because we have to lead on two fronts: we have to lead on a personal level as well as on the public level. Many people will not appreciate this level of crisis until they experience it.

- **People crisis**. During a people crisis, emotions tend to run high. Sometimes, these crises result from people in the church stirring up strife or creating confusion. At other times, it might be people on our staff who just aren't getting along. It's rare that a winner emerges from a people crisis, although there may be quite a few losers. If a senior leader from the church happens to get involved, the others somehow unanimously vote that leader as the big loser in that particular crisis.

> It's rare that a winner emerges from a people crisis, although there may be quite a few losers.

As leaders, we're going to receive many invitations to become involved in the people crises occurring within the church. If we have 100 people, we'll receive 100 invitations. Every time one brother enters into business with another brother and it doesn't work out, we're going to be called in to mediate.

Leadership in Peace and in War

- *In times of crisis, we need leaders. In times of peace, we need managers.*
- *Real leaders appear during times of crisis, or wartime.*
- *We may be barely swimming ahead of the sharks when someone throws us a rope. Remember that person on the other side of the crisis. During these stressful times, we can be so crisis driven that we can't identify potential leaders.*

The most important thing to remember in these situations is that our intervention should never become a substitute for people following the Word of God.

Matthew 18 tells us that people need to deal with these situations by themselves. It's only after they've made good-faith efforts to work through the issues that the church becomes involved at any level. That's important to remember because a lot of pastors become little more than referees in wrestling matches. When Dr. Brooks gets these calls, he always tells the people calling that it's not the church's job to act as a referee. He reminds them of

> ...a lot of pastors become little more than referees in wrestling matches.

the biblical mandates to walk in love and encourages them to fulfill the instructions of Matthew 18. Remember that every people crisis is an invitation. The best thing we can do is to decline these invitations and encourage people to act on the Word of God.

- **Public crisis.** A people crisis can develop into a public crisis. It becomes public when people in the church who are fighting begin drawing otherwise innocent folks into that crisis. That's when the senior pastor should consider stepping in to limit the amount of collateral damage.

Becoming involved requires a lot of wisdom. We don't want the intervention to be perceived as favoring any of the parties who may be involved. We need to be clear that we're only becoming involved because new people are being recruited; at this point, we want to limit the conflict to those who are currently involved. We want to be clear that we don't want any personal problems developing into church-wide problems.

> Remember that every people crisis is an invitation.

Dr. Brooks reminds people in his church that everyone has a right to mess up his or her own life. However, no one has the right to mess up the lives of others. The church doesn't need any more casualties from friendly fire within its ranks.

- **Problem crisis.** Sometimes, a crisis isn't caused by people; it's just part of life. It can be anything from a tight budget to someone learning that they have an untreatable disease. It's at these particular times that the pastor needs to be involved.

There are certain pastoral obligations that cannot and should not be delegated. When pastoring responsibilities are delegated in times of crisis, we trade away the equity we could build among our people. These types of crises are handled more by our presence than by our promise. In these

> A people crisis can develop into a public crisis.

situations, it's the shepherd's job to show up, to simply be present. During these times, our visibility will create security and whatever we say will be taken to heart.

We have to discern what's needed in each situation. At times, it's appropriate that we drive all night and show up in a hospital room. Not every situation calls for that type of response. It's obviously appropriate with board members or a staff member who has a serious illness in the family. We might elect to show up for a few minutes, a few hours, or maybe for a few days.

> ...no one has the right to mess up the lives of others.

There are other times when it's abundantly clear that our presence is required. Dr. Brooks has 30 families that started the church with him more than 20 years ago. By standing with these families whenever they need him, he's demonstrating an appropriate level of loyalty. It doesn't matter where he is; when these folks need him, he's going to be there. And when a family in the church lost someone in Iraq, he clearly felt the need to conduct the funeral.

> When pastoring responsibilities are delegated in times of crisis, we trade away the equity we could build among our people.

There are times when we simply have to pastor our flock; we don't get to delegate that.

- **Pressure crisis.** There will also be instances when the various pressures we're experiencing begin to accumulate on different levels. We may have a building program that's a month behind, which is going to create financial pressure if it's not completed soon. Along with that, we learn that one of our largest financial supporters is church shopping, and that a key staff member has accepted another post.

Taken individually, any of these situations would be taxing enough. When we're facing multiple pressures, we can be sure that others are watching us, using us as their example. People are watching us to determine how they will respond to these same pressures. We're being followed; that's what being a leader is about.

> There are times when we simply have to pastor our flock; we don't get to delegate that.

Differentiating among the various levels of crisis is easier when we consider the size and maturity of a church. When a church has 100 people, there's no such thing as a level to a crisis; every crisis is a big one. As the church grows, we can begin distinguishing the levels of crisis and of our involvement.

The Chinese characters for the word "crisis" are made up of two English words – *danger* and *opportunity*. Every time we encounter a crisis, we also have an opportunity. It can be an opportunity to model Christ-like leadership or to create equity and support. During a crisis, we'll build support faster than any other time. We'll also find that we can lose support more quickly than any other time.

> People are watching us to determine how they will respond to these same pressures. We're being followed; that's what being a leader is about.

That's why it's so important that we discern the appropriate actions rather than delegate these tasks. If we delegate, we're giving away our opportunity to create equity. In some places, if that equity is lost to another leader, we might be facing an entirely different crisis.

Building Support During a Crisis

No leader can know everything, do everything, or be everything. We need to have support – especially during times of crisis. Gaining needed support in the midst of a crisis is both an art and a science.

> The Chinese characters for the word "crisis" are made up of two English words – danger and opportunity.

During these situations, it is helpful to keep the following guidelines in mind:

- Deal with individuals rather than groups
- Apologize, when appropriate
- Control the timeline
- Manage our emotions

Deal with individuals rather than groups. Initially, the challenge is to keep a crisis from escalating while working to stabilize the situation. When there's tension between members over a church-related issue, attaining that stability is easier when we avoid group meetings. In groups, it's easy for emotions to run high, for misunderstandings to occur, and for negative attitudes to grow quickly.

> During a crisis, we'll build support faster than any other time. We'll also find that we can lose support more quickly than any other time.

Apologize, when appropriate. According to *The Harvard Business Review*, apologizing can be

---
No leader can know everything, do everything, or be everything.

---

a risky move. Depending on how it's delivered, an apology can be seen as a sign of weakness or as a sign of strength. Delivered correctly, however, an apology can be powerful enough to turn a crisis around. "A successful apology can turn enmity into personal and organizational triumph --whereas an apology that's too little, too late, or too transparently tactical can open the floodgates to individual and institutional ruin."[13]

What makes an apology effective? According to the article's author, Barbara Kellerman, leaders should apologize when one or more of these conditions apply[13]:

- An apology will serve an important purpose
- The offense carries serious consequences
- It's appropriate for the leader to assume responsibility
- The leader is the only one who can get the job done
- Saying something is less costly than saying nothing.

Control the timeline. In any crisis, time is the key to building consensus. An apology can help gain important time

---
...the challenge is to keep a crisis from escalating while working to stabilize the situation.

---

by defusing tension. In most cases, whoever controls the timeline of the situation will come out on top. When someone calls who is angry and says, "I want to see you now," that's an attempt to control the timeline. Taking control of the timeline in a peaceful fashion can change those dynamics and help to resolve the crisis.

Manage our emotions. When a crisis comes, it's usually a surprise, perhaps even a shock. This happened in 2 Chronicles, when Jehoshaphat received word that five armies were coming against him. Scripture says that fear was his first reaction to this accumulated pressure. His first reaction wasn't his last reaction, however. The next thing Jehoshaphat did was to seek the Lord. He immediately set to work on controlling his own emotions in the midst of this crisis.

Dr. Brooks' Perspective

During a crisis, most people will try to rope the pastor into meeting with them in groups. That's usually the quickest way to have that rope turn into a noose. Since it's easier to control the dynamics, I always choose to meet with people individually and stay within those boundaries as much as I can.

Because of our building program, we had a situation where a Sunday school class was displaced. I had been out of town, some of the work had been delayed, and a class wasn't able to use their room. When you lose your classroom, it's like losing your identity; it's a big thing to them.

The first thing I did was to call the individuals involved. When I reached them, I explained what happened, admitted that it was poor leadership on my part, and apologized. I also apologized personally to the entire class. It's hard to hang somebody who's coming to tell you that he's sorry.

When there's tension and I take the blame by apologizing, it deflects any responsibility from my staff and other decision makers and directs it towards me. In probably seventy percent of the church crises I've dealt with, I started off by apologizing. Even if people start out blaming a staff member, I'm eventually going to be blamed. The sooner that I step up to the plate, the sooner I'll begin to get people behind me.

When I work in a crisis situation I work at getting things as stable as possible during the first 48 hours. I've found that if I can get through the first 48 hours without things getting worse, it's usually an indication that I'm on my way to resolving things with God's help.

Emotions are always an important aspect of resolving a crisis. I've discovered that if I walk into a room and I'm angry, the only thing I'll succeed at is making everyone else mad at me. Sometimes, people sense those emotions and it adds to their own angry feelings. Being able to handle my own emotions is a major component of gaining support from others. I don't want them angry with me; I want them working with me.

Crisis Preparation

There's a difference between planning and preparation. As Dr. Chand mentions in his book *LadderShifts*, planning has a narrow focus, while preparation is broader in its scope. When you plan, you're trying to achieve some specific end; when you prepare, you're readying yourself for any possibility.

One of the major crises in Dr. Brooks' ministry involved an

automobile accident that took the lives of one young man's wife and his three children -- a three-year old, a one-year old, and a six-week old. We may not be facing a quadruple funeral, but we will be facing our own crises at some point. Think of the churches in the South that were struck by multiple hurricanes in 2006. They still managed to conduct services, even though they were without electricity, or in some cases, without buildings. They managed because they were prepared.

> A successful apology can turn enmity into personal and organizational triumph...

Since we don't know what specific crises are coming our way, it's impossible to plan for them. We can, however, take some steps to ensure that we're prepared:

- Over pack a suitcase
- Privately provide personal care
- Prepare a team of "first responders"
- Show up

Over pack a suitcase. Some people have difficulty packing for a short trip. Maybe you know someone who's arrived for a three-day weekend with three or four suitcases, a backpack, and some additional items. Perhaps they wanted to be

How to Get Better Prepared

1. Determine one or more worst-case scenarios, the worse possible situations that can occur.
2. Establish a potential response by thinking backwards from that scenario
3. Involve your staff in brainstorming potential action plans and needs.

Crisis Triage

A capable leader knows what vital signs to monitor during a crisis. Gently and firmly scrutinizing these points can prevent a crisis from escalating or move it toward resolution.

1. **Face the problems.** It's understandable to want to avoid pressure by ignoring unpleasant facts or situations. Unless we want to face similar situations later, it's best to summon our courage and deal with them now.

2. **Meet the needs.** Shorten the life of a crisis by taking an inventory of pressing financial, physical and emotional needs and prioritizing the results.

3. **Define the future.** In the midst of a storm, our present decisions or our inaction can define our future circumstances. We must trust that God is working together with us to enlarge our borders.

4. **Get help.** Asking for help is not a symptom of weakness but a sign of strength. We must know our limits and request assistance when needed.

5. **Answer questions.** Since complicated situations abound during a crisis, we cannot and should not come up with answers too quickly. We may have to patiently gather information, deliberate, and then decide.

6. **Inform the team.** Ignoring important stakeholders worsens a situation. If others are affected by or involved in addressing a crisis, ensure that they're informed about new developments or involved in making important decisions.

7. **Coordinate efforts and communication.** It's essential that "the right hand knows what the left hand is doing" to prevent unnecessary frustration and eliminate duplicate efforts.

8. **Respectfully communicate.** People on the periphery of a situation need to be respectfully informed. They may not be directly affected or involved, but keeping them in the loop prevents future problems.

9. **Evaluate operational communication needs.** When the crisis affects a large group, take the time to communicate about important matters to quell rumors or unanswered questions.

ready for any type of weather that came their way.

When it comes to a crisis, we can never be over packed or over prepared. In fact, if we haven't over prepared, we're likely going to find ourselves under prepared. We know that we're going to experience crises; we just don't know what will occur or when it will happen.

> There's a difference between planning and preparation.

There are some things we do know, however. We know that we're going to be preaching at least once on Sunday. Some of us know we're going to preach more than that. We may also know that we're conducting a mid-week Bible study. If we're not waiting until the day before a sermon or a Bible study to pull it together, we'll find that we're better prepared to handle a crisis.

Some of us live with too little margin. We're like people who live from paycheck to paycheck, never having anything saved for a rainy day. If we don't have an extra sermon ready or an extra service prepared, the day will come and we'll find that there's nothing in our savings account to draw on. When Dr. Chand was pastoring, he always had a backlog of three sermons and three Bible studies that he called his "just-in-case" file.

> We know that we're going to experience crises; we just don't know what will occur or when it will happen.

When we're over prepared for the things we know are coming, it makes it easier for us to handle whatever we aren't expecting.

Privately provide personal care. When Jesus raised Jairus' daughter, he didn't do it in front of the crowd in the house. Scripture says that "After he put them all out," he went to the child privately, with only her parents and the inner circle of his disciples[14].

Following Jesus' example, we'll find that we're better able to discern needs and handle emotions if we're not in the middle of a crowd of others affected by the crisis. This is how Dr. Brooks cared for the young man who'd lost his wife and children, by speaking with him privately. If there are other people who need attention, we can bring additional staff to help them.

> Some of us live with too little margin.

Prepare a team of "first responders." Police and firefighters are trained to treat the injured until adequate medical attention arrives; they're known as "first responders." Our staffs should also be ready to provide a similar response to a crisis within the church.

We must emphasize this same priority with our staff, underscoring the importance of being there for people who are truly hurting. The entire staff should understand that when this type of crisis occurs, it's "all hands on deck." You should never have to come looking for them. Knowing that Jesus came to heal the bruised and broken hearted, they're ready to do the same at a moment's notice.

> Eighty percent of success is showing up...

Show up. "Eighty percent of success is showing up," said Woody Allen. While his statement is somewhat tongue-in-cheek, we can't ignore the importance of simply being available for our people in crisis.

Scripture says that Jesus was moved by the needs of people who were like "sheep without a shepherd."[15] He didn't say that they were sheep without a leader or sheep without a communicator. They were sheep without a shepherd. Shepherds know how to be with their sheep; and being present is more important than knowing what to say.

When we're experiencing that weakness of not knowing how to respond, we can then be open for the Holy Spirit to work through us. We can pray the critical prayer, "Lord, I don't know what to say, so I desperately need your wisdom." We can exercise our faith in God's provision by simply standing in the gap, being available for God to work through us, being available to minister to those who are hurting, just as Jesus would.

...being present is more important than knowing what to say...

Teaching Points

- A crisis doesn't have to be an entirely negative experience.
- Leaders are often discovered in times of crisis.
- Not all problems are equal, nor do they deserve the same degree of attention.
- We should distinguish between the levels of crisis:
  - Personal crisis. Is fairly easy to recognize; may have a professional component.
  - People crisis. Emotions tend to run high. It's rare that a winner emerges.
  - Public crisis. Occurs when otherwise innocent folks are drawn into a fight.
  - Problem crisis. Sometimes a crisis is just part of life. We have to discern what's needed in each situation.
  - Pressure crisis. There are instances when various pressures begin to accumulate.
- During a crisis, we will build support faster than any other time.
- Gaining support is easier when adhering to certain guidelines:
  - Deal with individuals rather than groups.
  - Apologize, when appropriate.
  - Control the timeline.
  - Manage our emotions.
- Preparing for a crisis readies us for any possibility.
- We can take steps to ensure we're prepared:
  - Prepare in advance for sermons and other services.
  - Provide personal care privately.
  - Have our staff ready to respond.
  - Be available to people in crisis.

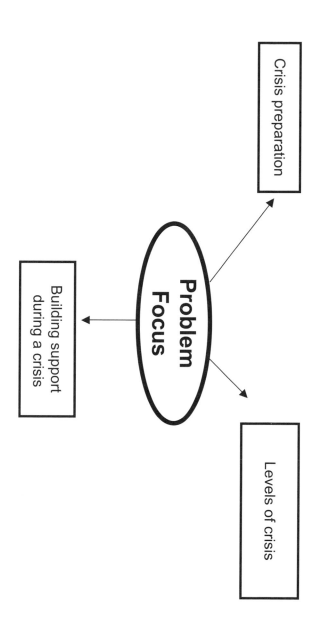

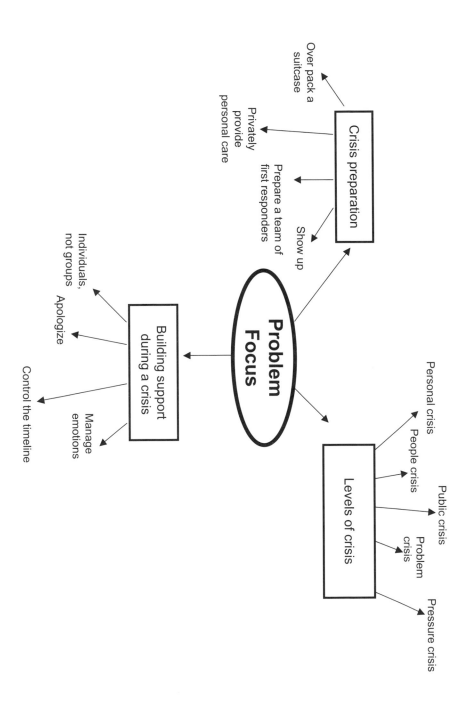

Afterword

Have you ever found yourself at a place where you knew that you were emotionally and spiritually drowning? Even if no one else around you sensed the place of emergency that you were in, you knew that if nothing happened, if nothing changed, if someone didn't step in, you would go under. If you have ever been in this place, after reading *Ladder Focus* you will agree with me when I say that this book surely is a lifeline of hope, direction and encouragement. Maybe you haven't been at that place, or you just aren't there right now. *Ladder Focus* still should prove valuable to you as an instrument that moves you from being reactive to being proactive in your ministerial goals, vision and processes.

As a pastor of almost 25,000 people, celebrating my 20th year pastoral anniversary, I find myself often in a place of transition. God never allows me to get too comfortable where I am and is constantly challenging me to grow, to shift and to change. I often rely heavily on the knowledge, integrity and experience of both Dr. Chand and Dr. Brooks. I consider them both to be a part of my strategic team of advisors, whether through personal contact, through me simply listening to messages they have taught, or reading the books they have written. I am often amazed at how effortlessly it seems that they walk in their gifting and how they have both truly tapped into the essence of their calling.

It is my prayer that you did not simply read this work for information but that you read it for life. The authors talk about the different ways that God speaks to us. One way that He often speaks to me is by opening my heart to the wisdom of men and women of God. God has certainly spoken a timely Word to Dr. Chand and Dr. Brooks and when God speaks directly to you or though His people, He is speaking life. Do not allow yourself to simply check *Ladder Focus* off your "things to read" list. Take your time to truly process what you have learned. Reread it. Apply the principles. Meet with your ministerial team and discuss it. Reread it again. Although I firmly believe that experience is one of our best teachers, I also believe that we deal with, go through and struggle in areas that we do not have to. Allow the experiences of the authors to serve as a warning to the potential mines that may lay ahead and allow it to serve as a roadmap to discerning and reaching your destiny.

May we all move from low thinking to truly understanding the big picture and being strategic in our ministry, our businesses and our personal lives. May we truly look honestly at where we are and where God has called us to be so that we will continue to operate effectively and truly walk in the authority of sons and daughters of the King. *Ladder Focus* is a vital tool in ensuring that we are about our Father's Business. I look forward to hearing of the lives that have been rescued and restored through this project.

Bishop Eddie L. Long
Senior Pastor
New Birth Missionary Baptist Church

Bibliography

1.   2 Samuel 5:22

2   Ephesians 1:17-18

3   Ephesians 5:21

4   Philippians 3:13

5   1 Peter 5:2

6.   Proverbs 27:19

7.   Habakkuk 2:2

8.   Acts 2:47

9.   John 15:16

10.   1 Samuel 22:2

11.   2 Corinthians 4:13

12.   Proverbs 20:24

13.   "When Should a Leader Apologize--and When Not?" *Harvard Business Review*, April 2006.

14.   Mark 5:40

15.   Matthew 9:36

About Dr. Samuel R. Chand

As a *Dream Releaser*, Sam Chand serves pastors, ministries, and businesses as a leadership architect and change strategist. He is a popular and much sought after speaker for churches, corporations, leadership and ministry conferences, and other leadership development seminars.

In 1973, while a student at Beulah Heights Bible College, Sam Chand served as janitor, cook, and dishwasher. He graduated and was ordained in the ministry in 1977 and went on to serve as an associate and senior pastor in several churches. Sixteen years later, he returned to BHBC to serve as the president for the next 14 years. Under his leadership, BHBC became one of the fastest growing bible colleges in America experiencing a 600% increase in student growth, an enrollment of approximately 700 students from over 400 churches, 45 denominations, and 32 countries. Beulah Heights Bible College (now Beulah Heights University) is also the country's largest predominantly African-American Bible college. He also served the university as chancellor, and now as president emeritus.

Currently, Dr. Chand ...

- Consults with businesses and large churches on leadership and capacity enhancing issues
- Conducts nation-wide leadership conferences
- Presents at international leadership conferences with Dr. John Maxwell's ministry of EQUIP
- Serves on the board of EQUIP, with the goal to equip 50 million leaders worldwide

- Oversees and leads Bishop Eddie L. Long's leadership development initiatives through Father's House, Spirit & Truth and other leadership development events
- Is on the Board of New Birth Academy and Beulah Heights University.
- Dr. Chand has authored and published six books, which are used worldwide for leadership development. His books include:

LadderShifts: New Realities, Rapid Change, Your Destiny describes how to deal with sudden changes and unanticipated demands.

What's Shakin' Your Ladder: 15 Challenges All Leaders Face advice for leaders on how to overcome the things that are blocking them.

Who Moved Your Ladder: Your Next Bold Move This book provides pragmatic guidelines for dealing with transitions in life and leadership.

Who's Holding Your Ladder A reminder to that the most critical decision leaders will make is selecting who will be on their leadership team.

FUTURING: Leading your Church into Tomorrow This book is helps leaders to begin a future oriented dialog about their organization.

Failure: The Womb of Success a compilation of stories on how to overcome failure with contributions from twenty respected Christian leaders.

Chand's educational background includes an honorary Doctor of Divinity from Heritage Bible College, a Master of Arts in Biblical Counseling from Grace Theological Seminary, a Bachelor of Arts in Biblical Education from Beulah Heights Bible College.

Dr. Chand shares his life and love with his wife Brenda, two daughters Rachel and Deborah and granddaughter Adeline.

Being raised in a pastor's home in India has uniquely equipped Dr. Chand to share his passion – that of mentoring, developing and inspiring leaders to break all limits—in ministry and the marketplace.

For further information please contact:

Samuel R. Chand Consulting
950 Eagles Landing Parkway, Suite 295
Stockbridge, GA 30281
www.samchand.com

LEADERSHIP RESOURCES
BY SAMUEL R. CHAND

FUTURING:
Leading Your Church into Tomorrow

The message will never change. But the methods to present the message can and must change to reach a realm of churchgoers. Forty-four specific areas that are changing in the church today.

WHO'S HOLDING YOUR LADDER?
Leadership's Most Critical Decision
—Selecting Your Leaders

Those around you, not you, the visionary, will determine your success.

WHO MOVED YOUR LADDER?
Your Next Bold Move

Taking the next bold move is not easy—but you finally admit, "I have no choice. I have to jump!"

This book will equip you for that leap.

WHAT'S SHAKIN' YOUR LADDER?
15 Challenges All Leaders Face

Take an in-depth look at the common challenges that all leaders face, and benefit from practical advice on facing and overcoming the things that are blocking you from being the best you can be.

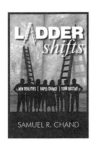

LADDER SHIFTS
New Realities - Rapid Change - Your Destiny

No leader is immune to the shifting circumstances and events that can challenge or stymie their professional or organizational progress. Advance warning of these oncoming storms, together with adequate preparation, can mean the difference between disaster and success.

CHANGE:
Leading Change Effectively

- Healthy confessions for those leading change
- Tradition and traditionalism
- Responding to seasons and times
- Levels of change
- Factors that facilitate or hinder change
- Steps for positive change
- Selling your idea
- Creating a team
- Personal challenges of the leader leading change

DEVELOPING A LEADERSHIP CULTURE

- Why do leaders do what they do?
- Why and when leaders make changes?
- Vision levels of people
- Contemporary leadership
- Why leaders fail
- Qualities of a successful leader

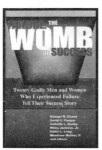

FAILURE:
The Womb of Success

- Failure is an event not a person
- Failure is never final
- Twenty leaders tell their stories

FORMATION OF A LEADER

Spiritual Formation
- Born to lead
- Security or sabotage

Skill Formation
- The day Moses became a leader

Strategic Formation
- Live the life you were meant to live
- Mentoring: How to invest your life in others

FUTURING:
Leading Your Church Into Tomorrow

- Futuring leadership traits
- Challenges for the 21st century
- How ministry will change in the next 3-7 years
- Motivational fuels for 21st century church
- Addition versus multiplication of leaders

12 SUCCESS FACTORS FOR AN ORGANIZATION

- Handling Complexity
- Completion
- Lead and Manage People
- Executional Excellence

WHAT KEEPS PASTORS UP AT NIGHT

- Do my people get the vision?
- Are things getting done?
- How is the team working together?
- Do I have the team I need to get it done?

WHO'S HOLDING YOUR LADDER?

- Ladder holders determine the Leader's ascent
- Selecting your ladder holders
- Different ladder holders for different levels
- Qualities of a good ladder holder
- Development of ladder holders
- Leaders versus Managers
- Turning ladder holders into ladder climbers

WHO MOVED YOUR LADDER?
Your Next Bold Move

- What's wrong with me?
- What's wrong with my ladder?
- What's going on?
- What happened to the challenge?
- Where's the thrill of achievement?

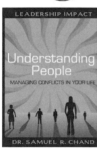

UNDERSTANDING PEOPLE:
Managing Conflicts in Your Ministry

- What conflict does
- High maintenance relationships
- Predictable times of conflict
- Levels of conflict
- Diffusing conflict
- Conflict resolution

HOW TO ORDER RESOURCES

WRITE
Samuel R. Chand Consulting
950 Eagles Landing Parkway, Suite 295
Stockbridge, GA 30281

WEBSITE
www.samchand.com

NOTES
1. BULK purchase (10 or more) rates available.
2. Credit cards & checks accepted

LEADERSHIP RESOURCES
BY GERALD BROOKS

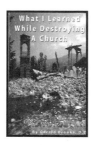

WHAT I LEARNED WHILE DESTROYING A CHURCH:

In a world that seldom provides an opportunity for second chances, it is critical that we learn from the experiences of others. This book walks you through the eight mistakes that destroyed my first church.

JESUS ON LEADERSHIP

Jesus Christ is the ultimate example of leadership. Explore the foundational leadership principles exemplified through our Savior's life and ministry.

PAUL ON LEADERSHIP

Two thousand years ago, the Apostle Paul began equipping leaders with the principles of effective ministry. These principles are just as relevant and imperative for us today as they were when Paul recorded them.

THE OLD TESTAMENT ON LEADERSHIP

There are no new problems under the sun, nor are there new answers. The God of the past is the God of the present—and He who brought us through yesterday will guide us into tomorrow.

BUILDING BLOCKS OF LEADERSHIP

All levels of leaders will benefit from this practical guide, which offers insights into some basic yet frequently overlooked principles of leading others.

THE EMOTIONS OF A LEADER

Develop the necessary skills to handle the often-overlooked emotional side of leadership from this practical guide, regardless of your leadership experience.

HOW TO ORDER RESOURCES

FOR MORE INFORMATION ON:
- Books
- Prices
- Monthly leadership subscriptions
- Leadership roundtables and registrations
- How to purchase leadership materials
- Available ministry resources

Call 972-985-1112, extension 105

MONTHLY LEADERSHIP SUBSCRIPTIONS
Get *two free books* when you sign up
for Gerald Brooks
Monthly Leadership Subscription

LEADERSHIP CONFERENCE
Join hundreds other pastors.
Attend a Leadership Conference
with Pastor Brooks at Grace Outreach Center!

ROUNDTABLE
Attend a leadership roundtable in your area

For information, visit www.growingothers.com

Notes

NOTES

NOTES

Notes

NOTES

NOTES

NOTES

NOTES

NOTES

NOTES